EMBRACING GOD

DAVID SWARTZ

HARVEST HOUSE PUBLISHERS
Eugene, Oregon 97402

EMBRACING GOD

Copyright © 1994 by Harvest House Publishers
Eugene, Oregon 97402

Library of Congress Cataloging-in-Publication Data

Swartz, David.
   Embracing God / David Swartz.
      p.   cm.
   ISBN 1-56507-125-5
   1. Christian life—1960–   I. Title.
BV4501.2.S875   1994
248.4—dc20   93-34312
                                          CIP

Printed in the United States of America.

94 95 96 97 98 99 – 10 9 8 7 6 5 4 3 2 1

For Gay:

If all else would slip away
but for your love
that has dignified my life
for these twenty years,
I could still stand straight
knowing I was a
rich man.

Acknowledgments

One of the joys of the writing process involves the way lives intertwine in the process. That was certainly true here. The good people at Harvest House had confidence in the project that humbly kept my shoulder to the wheel. Eileen Mason kept the focus sharp with very insightful, constructive criticisms. Steve Miller walked me through steps toward the deadline and fine-tuned the book through the editorial process—my gratitude for his patience and grace.

The people of Bethel Baptist Church prayed us through the writing, and some provided meals so writing and typing could go on. I'm grateful that God has woven our lives together, and in a tight spot I would covet their prayers more than a squadron of tanks. Bonnie Mazzola, my secretary, went her usual fifth extra mile in preparing the manuscript and covering the office. So much happens because of her unseen excellence; the book is an example.

I mention Steve and Karen, my children, to say how much more important they are than any book. The satisfaction of heart they provide as they have grown into friends honors me deeply. Their ear for God's voice and heart for His kingdom convince me that the greatest marks for the kingdom of God in our family will yet be struck after their father's books vanish and his voice falls silent. And I rejoice in this.

And for Gay. I wrote this book somewhat selfishly, since another book dedicated to her went out of print. If all this book were to do is provide a billboard for another dedication, that alone would have ennobled these pages more than I could hope.

—David Swartz

Contents

1

⚜

What's Wrong?

Red neon, frosted in the deli window by winter wind off the lake, framed every face from where I sat nursing a muffin and coffee. These were busy people like me, with so much to do that we were buying our groceries at 5:30 in the morning. The mental pile of tasks crying to be done has seemingly left us no other time but this. Faces furrow and frown, I assume wincing into the bite of the wind.

But later, in glaring lights over grapefruit and oranges, their faces haven't changed. Maybe they don't enjoy the predawn dash from a warm bed to the temporary womb of a warm car just for some eggs and corn chips any more than I do. Deep lines etched around eyes hint that some of these people clutch winter in their hearts all the time.

It's one thing to see these faces over bagels in the supermarket deli at five in the morning, but quite another to watch people whose souls are gripped by winter enter and leave the church seemingly no warmer than when they came.

Our times brim over with people in pain. Eyes downcast or empty tip us off that someone carries something heavy. Wounded by life or withered and cheated by life that never materialized, countless people mull over their hurt, waiting for the traffic light to change or the connecting flight to leave. Sometimes human pain is like waking up with a third arm: We don't know where it came from, but it's there. Many people can't do much more than carry it around. They're too preoccupied and busy to be healed. Maybe they didn't know how it could happen, or despaired that it even would.

Making No Sense

Something is not making sense in American Christianity today. In the case of millions of people it seems to make no difference in daily life to be Christian. As a result, Christians are not always making much difference in the lives of others.

On the surface we certainly seem to be doing well. If we stand on the sidewalk in front of the headquarters of many denominations or ministries, it's hard not to be impressed with the institutional solidity and respectability that radiates from the tinted windows, sculpted concrete, and landscaped grounds. Christian publishing is no longer the back room enterprise it once was. In quality, volume, and sales, Christian publishing and music ventures now seem to be good investments to secular companies and conglomerates, who buy them up as subsidiaries.

Even our bookstores don't look much like the one I remember from college days, where a retired missionary sold books from a card table on her sun porch. A walk across the campus of many Christian colleges or seminaries gives the same impression. Christian celebrities and artists appear on network secular television and in other ways gain nationwide attention. While this doesn't apply to every church, ministry, business, or artist, no one can argue that Christian institutions and enterprises have flourished over the last 50 years.

So what doesn't make sense? Many Christians, both individuals and families, make all the right "Christian" moves without seeing a corresponding and resulting effect. We belong to good churches that believe and teach the Bible. Although we may struggle with consistency, we strive to read the Bible and pray. Our marriages and kids have been made as bulletproof as we can manage with the help of James Dobson and Bill Gothard. Our car radios are locked into the station broadcasting our favorite Bible teacher. We're galvanizing our kids against the corrosion of secular humanism and gratuitous violence with all the right videos, video games, and praise tapes. But something is missing: Grace is not penetrating down where deep hurt, sin, and infection have oozed and scabbed over for years.

Too many of us are musty-spirited people. We come in many sizes and shapes. One of these is the fractured life under plaster. The well-scrubbed, dignified face we see on Sundays is paneling; reality is underneath and will never come out. Maybe that's because the church isn't supposed to be the place for things like personal pain or feelings to show. Even if it is, many churchgoers won't risk it for a hundred reasons. A lot of those people sitting around us on Sundays looking fine really aren't.

Some hurt openly because there's no way to keep it quiet. Public sin, marital breakdown, or children out of control broadcast loudly of failure, both real and imagined. How hard it is to sit in a worship service and focus your thoughts on God when it seems like everyone's thoughts are focused on *you!* When the hurt splashes out in the open for the rest of the congregation to see, it gets harder to come at all. Christianity can seem like a deflated balloon—reality, but a limp one without much comfort.

Some people attend the church because they are loyal to the organization. They are usually older and were taught from their childhood that faithfulness meant coming to church. These are dear people. Churches exist today because these people came, did the menial tasks, and pledged an extra five dollars a month for the building program. Those respectable and successful institutions I mentioned earlier owe it all to these folks. But loyalty to the church is all some of them know. Speak of the grace of God penetrating deeply into our lives and you may notice them smile rather woodenly and even nod. But a quizzical look haunts their eyes because Christian buzzwords and clichés describe spiritual realities they haven't tasted for a long time, if ever.

Some pass briefly through the church's doors, wanting quality without being willing to pay the price. Christian maturity and victory cannot be microwaved. Our hectic, busy society reduces everything to a technique and the bottom line. Books and seminars that promise quick fixes or four easy steps to this or that may flirt with us and tempt us. But patterns of sin, weakness, and error deeply ingrained over years simply aren't going to vanish that easily.

Some people whip through churches the way they whisk through the mall. Seeking God isn't so much their aim as seeking happiness, well-being, professional success, or any one of a host of items on their personal agenda. They are consumers who look to shop around for the best array of goods and services instead of seeking involvement in community with God's people.

Some churchgoers are disillusioned. They were really hungry once and straining at the leash to grow. But they weren't sure how to go about it and didn't get much help. Eventually hope began to flicker that it might happen at all. In some large and full churches the erosion of hope goes on silently. Cavities of hearts that once craved joy, meaning, and purpose now lie empty and dark. The sense of despair of many such people runs especially deep because it rises in the setting of a Christian life where all the furniture of faith may be properly arranged. These people come every Sunday but are quietly hanging by their fingernails. If things don't change for them soon, the church will be poorer of some who might have been choice servants of the Lord.

Not Always This Way

It hasn't always been this way. The lives of those first people to follow Jesus Christ laid open a "no-holds-barred" account called the Acts of the Apostles. As a group, they presented a pretty unsophisticated picture. They had no complete Bible, owned neither buildings nor property, worshiped without organs or hymnals as we know them, and never imagined the results of technology we enjoy today. But they seemed to be finding some things that elude us. They had an unshakable assurance of God's forgiveness that left no residual film of lingering guilt.

This made them exuberantly bold. The unraveling effects of their sin were reversed, their lives being reknit from the inside out. Peace and joy that didn't depend on the fickleness of daily circumstances touched every aspect of their lives. Beyond the slaying of dragons within and rising above the press of externals, God actually indwelt their personalities and beings; they truly knew Him. They embodied three things that Jesus said would always be true of His disciples: "They would be absurdly happy, completely fearless, and in constant trouble."[1]

They were an infectious bunch. Something alluring drew other people to see what made them tick, to see what made their life together throb with vitality. People even lined up to marvel at their dying. The world pressed like kids against a candy store window to stare enviously, even hungrily, at two things.

First, they saw truth. Whatever else it was, these early Christians had all of creation, the core of reality, by the tail in knowing Jesus Christ. In embracing Him the Christians had sunk the supports of their lives into the bedrock undergirding the universe.

Second, the world saw a wholeness of body, mind, and spirit rising in the lives of these ordinary people that defied human explanation. While they were by no means perfect, these Christians saw destructive behavioral and relational patterns broken and replaced with life directions and quality far beyond the mere healing of old scars and wounds.

Who wouldn't want all this? But we're torn. People in other cultures capture monkeys for food as well as for pets. They put peanuts in hollowed-out coconuts and leave the coconuts where the monkeys readily find them. The monkeys reach in to get the peanuts, but the hole in the coconut is sized just right so they can't remove their hand while it's full. Many monkeys would rather try to drag the coconut away than let go of the peanuts. Their greed costs them their freedom, sometimes their lives.

What We Want or What We Need?

In counseling people, I've observed that while many in serious trouble may not necessarily know what they need, they always know what they want. The shipwrecks of too many lives, marriages, and families give mute evidence that some people can't let go of their wants to embrace their needs. We would rather clutch peanuts, even if it means bondage or death, than run to freedom. God, because He loves us more deeply than we can fathom, cannot bear to idly let this happen. He has bound Himself as our Father to provide our needs. Even more, He aspires for our lives to be far more than a hobo's stew of changing dreams and goals or dashed hopes.

God has His way of helping us let go of whatever the "peanuts" may be in our life—even the seemingly good or harmless things that keep us from freedom and vitality. It's called *brokenness*. Brokenness from God's hand does not describe life beating us up. It does not mean that we're damaged goods beyond repair, scarred by the sins, faults, and foibles of others. It means that God insistently compels us to let go of the peanuts to embrace the glory of His will.

Sometimes He must peel our grip loose one finger at a time. At other times a whack on the wrist is what's needed to make us drop everything and run to Him. Then at times God dangles the treasures of what Paul referred to as the unsearchable riches of Christ in front of us like jewels glistening in the sunlight. Compared to what God holds out to us, even our most cherished dreams and wants look like nothing more than . . . peanuts.

Chisel of Glory

Spiritual brokenness is not to be dreaded but embraced; we're not to flinch as God's hand draws near. Instead, it is a cherished trophy for those who have discovered in awe that God's love in Jesus Christ blazed up even more fiercely the more their blackness was brought to light. It is the cost gladly paid by those who long to know God so intensely that they are willing to endure the heat of His holiness— only to find that holiness cloaking them like a shimmering robe. It is a badge of honor identifying a common people across centuries and cultures who have never really belonged or fit in, being wayfarers and strangers, because their deepest hopes and hungers could only be satisfied in God.

In Christ's trusted and loving hand, brokenness becomes the chisel that etches His glory and image into my spirit, the plane that peels only to smooth. It is the transforming privilege of His cross pressed into my rebellious clay. But the results are worth it. Because of Christ my life makes sense; I don't have to grapple with my identity. In Christ I know who I am. And I live knowing that who I am is defined and protected by His Word. My life also has meaning that is unshakable in that I need not grope for it among things and ventures of my own construction. In Christ my life and soul strives toward that for which it was created: to know, love, and serve Him. Lastly, I know that in Christ I am cherished by God to the very depths of my soul.

Brokenness does not just come crashing into our lives in jagged thrusts like lightning. In reality it is sprinkled across every field of concern in our lives. Those who strive hotly after Christ will encounter brokenness at every turn. Seasoned by grace, we should begin to recognize it as a valuable companion. In the following pages we will track its footprints over every spiritual terrain imaginable. One word of warning is in order: We may not emerge from these pages the way we went in. George Mallone wrote that these people in Acts were "people whose bellies were full of God and nothing else."[2] We might become one of them.

The Acts of the Apostles is intentionally incomplete. Paul, Peter, John, Barnabas, Philip, Priscilla, and the others fade into the mist. That's because the story isn't over. It's *our* turn to have Jesus Christ live His life through us as He did through them—all under the watching eyes of people who crave joy and meaning, and in their innermost being haven't dreamed of how much God loves them. We don't need to cast longing glances at the first century. Jesus Christ stands unshackled by time and is poised to write the latest installment of Acts in our lives.

If anything said up till now has caused a flame to shoot up in your heart where there seemed to be only dust and ashes, know that God Himself has placed the spark there. In spite of sin, failure, and possibly years squandered in mediocrity, if you genuinely desire to burn with the love of Christ at the core of your being, Jesus Christ has no intention of disappointing you.

2

*The Touch
We Miss*

oss Hart, the fine American playwright, tells of walking down Lexington Avenue in New York City with his father. The sparkle of Christmas as only a young boy could see it hung in the air. As they turned onto Lexington, the street buzzed with activity. Deliverymen unloaded crates of geese that would marinate in plum sauce on someone's table. The roasting smell of chestnuts so hot they had to be tossed from hand to hand to cool pungently teased every nose. Windows were draped in holly, pine, tinsel, and ribbon.

But as young Hart took all this in, his eyes were already searching the stands and carts of vendors who lined the street with piles of toys and anything a child might want. As they passed chemistry sets and toy trains, Moss piped up that these would be great gifts for a boy to get. His father said nothing, but as they moved on he would pick up this toy or that as though it might be something desirable. But Moss had visions of chemistry sets and trains in his head.

Embracing God

This went on until they passed the last vendor and stood silently on the corner. The sound of a few coins jingling in his father's pocket broke the awkward silence— and then Moss Hart knew. Those coins were all his father could scrape together for Christmas. He saw a hopeless empty pain wash over his father's eyes as the man stared over the boy's head and down the street. Hart wanted to reach out and touch his father's hand to say, "It's all right. I love you. It doesn't matter." But they returned wordlessly to the house and the incident never came up again.

The 12 inches that stood between Moss Hart and his father on a New York sidewalk might as well have been 12 miles. Although the urge to touch and be touched deeply cried out in both father and son, "we were not on that basis," Moss Hart later recalled.

Every human being is a person of vast inner space. Cultural and socioeconomic distinctions make no difference. We tend to categorize and label people according to the little pieces we see of them. But there is infinitely more than meets the eye to both the well-heeled matron who came to my office promoting fine art auctions and our homeless friends who live off sandwiches from the day-care center.

We have twin difficulties as we take a serious look within. Our inner space is so vast that we have difficulty charting or understanding it ourselves. Some of it hurts; some of it breeds shame; much is incomprehensible. But a second struggle lies in finding another person who can be trusted to penetrate our inner space. What if those we trust enough to let in are insensitive to the holy ground they stand on? We fear being vulnerable that deep inside; we sense a nakedness of spirit that makes us pull our defenses tight around us until they sometimes harden into a shell.

Craving to Know and Be Known

Cravings ambush us at times. Sometimes a Snickers bar from a convenience store late at night takes care of it.

But some cravings run a lot deeper than a junk-food fix. They lie ingrained deeply in this human fabric of ours and yearn strongly to be met beneath the whirl and rush of the surface concerns of life. They rise from our depths as we lie awake at two in the morning, staring absentmindedly out a window or leafing through the family photo album. One of these is a cavity lying tucked away in a far recess of every heart that longs to be filled. We crave intimacy; we yearn to know and be known.

To know in this way means to grasp the essence of what is known, to understand to the very core. My brother-in-law has studied wilderness living. He understands the wildernesses of different climates and sees volumes where most people see nothing. Take animals, for instance. He knows their mating, feeding, and living habits right down to being able to read much from their droppings. He often returns from his outings looking as if he's been right down their burrows. Intimacy means sometimes going where others might not choose and paying close attention to things others don't care about. To know and to be known presses this on us.

As we saw with Moss Hart and his father, our need for intimacy is neither a merely casual nor a purely intellectual pursuit. It's an intensely *personal* one. We give the impression of wanting our space. Six-foot-high privacy fences surround most houses where I live. Strangers share small tables at the deli during lunch hour, saying not so much as a word to each other over gyros or corned beef. But the same guy who might never come from behind the privacy fence to ring my doorbell will buttonhole me for 45 minutes outside the 7-Eleven to talk, to have a human ear listen.

We are a society, a world, of fractured and lonely people. I exist—but unless someone understands me beyond the external boundaries of my existence and on into my inner space, I will live in the grip of crippling loneliness. If this longing for intimacy, to be known, is there, where did it come from? This means asking questions bigger than we are. Instead of becoming introspectively preoccupied, we need to look beyond ourselves. Who else besides man inhabits the universe? If the answer is that no one is there, it doesn't matter where our longing for intimacy came from. If we are alone in the universe, all talk of needing intimacy is but a narcotic to numb a harsh and empty reality—a blanket we roll up in for some temporary warmth against the cold of cosmic loneliness.

The Bible is clear: Outside, undergirding and woven through all existence, *God is*. Genesis 1:1 says, "In the beginning God created the heavens and the earth." Not a word, not a breath, is spent on some explanation of how God came to be. His existence is never proven; it is assumed. Behind all there is lies a mind, a Person. We are no accident, fluke, or evolutional happenstance. "God said, 'Let Us make man in Our image, according to Our likeness'" (Genesis 1:26). Humans are intentional creations of God and bear the stamp of the family character.

While being created in God's image bristles with implications, one of these is that mankind has the hunger for intimacy because it is innately coded into us by God's design. He Himself is relational. God is a Person—not a philosophical abstract, an impersonal cosmic force, or mere spiritual energy. The Christian doctrine of the Trinity underscores this by describing God as the Father, the Son, and the Holy Spirit—one God expressed in three Persons, coequal and interrelating. Within God's Person lies the capacity for relationship, for intimacy, to know and be known. We desire to know and be known because our spirit is cast in the genetics of our Creator; we are created in His image. And while we certainly need intimate human contact, God Himself is the One who stands as the primary object of our desire for intimacy and its richest satisfaction.

Who Gets the Keys to My Heart?

There are no secure people—not completely. It's just a matter of where our insecurities happen to lie. Mine may be different from yours. And even mine have a fluid quality about them; they shift and change as I grow older. My longing for intimacy, especially with God, is like the longing to reach out to grasp a beautiful rose. The beauty and fragrance of the rose alluringly draw me, but the thorns make me deliberate and hesitant. Intimacy is risky, even downright frightening. I have control over how much of the real me my family and friends can know. But God, if He is who the Bible says, is bigger than I am. By virtue of strength and power, He knows everything about me whether I tell Him or not. No privacy fence shields any aspect of my life from Him. What is God's disposition toward what He knows?

John says twice that "God is love" (1 John 4:8,16). Love is the foundational expression of the heart of the Creator of the universe. His love is no indulgent sentimentality. Human love can be conditional and can be wounded unto death, but God's love, although through it He becomes vulnerable to great pain, is always wonderfully blind to cost and consequences. He cannot be hurt or shocked into not loving. While God judges, He never does so in a wounded backlash of spurned or disregarded love. So while I simultaneously long for, yet draw back from, intimacy with God and other people, the first plank that helps extricate me from the quicksand of my insecurities is knowing that God, who knows all about me, loves me.

But that's not enough. A college roommate and I stood at the edge of a frozen pond one January day. He assured me that the ice was thick enough to hold us. Since he was so certain, I suggested that he go first. God's loving nature may mean nothing more to me than that He won't spill the beans about what He knows. What it comes to baring hearts, God went first in reaching toward us by telling us about His innermost thoughts and revealing His heart— often to a humanity that couldn't, at times, care less. Theologians call this the doctrine of revelation.

Some things about me you would never know without my telling. I love jazz and enjoy making balloon sculptures.

At meals, I eat one thing at a time, saving the meat and drink for last. We can't really know anyone unless they exercise trust and reveal themselves to us. God took the lead; He went first. Revelation means that God revealed Himself and that, if He had not taken the initiative in doing so, we could know nothing left to ourselves. He has crossed the threshold of relationship toward us by making Himself known in myriad ways.

Three demand our special attention.

What God Has Made

God shows us what He is like through what He has made. Just as Genesis takes no time to prove God's existence, neither does it feel obligated to tell us how God actually created everything. Were Genesis nothing more than a technical manual detailing the specifications and schematics of creation, the most brilliant scientific minds today would be pompously foolish to believe they could comprehend it. The apostle Paul wrote, ". . . since the creation of the world His invisible attributes, His eternal power and divine nature, have been clearly seen, being understood through what has been made" (Romans 1:20). A physical world showing the marks of abuse and a humanity scarred by sin may not reflect perfectly the Creator's image. But like a masterpiece smeared with layers of cheap varnish, the touches of a gifted guided hand are still there to be seen.

Existence itself says not only that God *exists* but that He is a craftsman without peer. Artists do incredible things with paint, clay, wood, or stone. In creating the world, God did incredible things with *nothing*. Creation emanated from the empty vacuum of complete chaos. As I cower like a rabbit down a hole deciding whether I want to risk intimacy with this God, He reaches toward me and says in effect, "Look around at nature. All this came from sheer nothingness." As my life has had its plunges into seemingly irretrievable chaos, my ears prick up and I soften toward reaching back.

What God Has Done

God takes the first step in reaching out to us through what He has done. We live many days at the bottom of dry wells with no rope. Our situations seem to have no solutions, no hope of deliverance or change. So we plunge on from day to day somewhat numbed by our hectic routines but still quietly desperate, still silently despairing. Love is easy to talk about, but actions always test the mettle of love. The biblical account of the escape of the children of Israel from Egypt is a lot more than a cracking good story. A people numbering possibly in the hundreds of thousands suffered under oppression at the hands of one of the most powerful nations on the earth. Through an incredible series of direct interventions, God broke the spine of the oppressors, brought His people out of Egypt, and guided every step night and day. He provided food and protection continually until He led them to a new land. God says, "If I can break the chains that fetter an entire nation, I think I can find a rope that will reach the bottom of your well."

But that was so long ago, and on a scale seemingly so vast, that it's hard to connect with it meaningfully now. Meet Elijah, the prophet. Biblical prophets are a scruffy, unapproachable bunch. They seem strong, invincible, cut from very different cloth than we are. But the man of 1 Kings 19 is so much like we are. In the wake of the greatest triumph of Elijah's prophetic life, an evil queen threatened his life. Elijah ran because he was afraid. Fear, as it often does, bred self-pity and maybe even a touch of shame.

In response, God allowed rest and provided nourishment—all without whipping Elijah for his weakness. God replenished Elijah's strength and recalibrated him for meaningful, even strategic, service. While part of us deeply desires intimacy with God, vandals like shame, fatigue, and self-pity may paralyze us from reaching out and may even nearly extinguish the desire to do so. But God says through what He does that He still reaches out, still takes the first step toward us.

Who God Has Given

God shows us most clearly the bent of His heart through Jesus Christ, His Son.

> God, after He spoke long ago to the fathers in the prophets in many portions and in many ways, in these last days has spoken to us in His Son, whom He appointed heir of all things, through whom also He made the world. And He is the radiance of His glory and the exact representation of His nature, and upholds all things by the word of His power. When He made purification of sins, He sat down at the right hand of the Majesty on high (Hebrews 1:1-3).

God became a man who stood right in front of us, not in some churchy setting, but in the gritty and exhausting arena of everyday life to show us what He was like. Jesus' teachings, healings, dealings with people—even His death on the cross—show anyone taking a moment to look the deepest concerns of God's heart. *Intimacy:* We long for it with God and others. But disclosure means exposure, and exposure means vulnerability. Yet God goes first; the Bible is His diary where His heart is bare on every page. His love for us and disclosure to us make Him vulnerable. But He always thinks the risk is worth it.

What God Really Wants

We tend to see life through the lenses of our needs and wants. My need for love and intimacy means finding the right other person to meet my need. How difficult it is to escape the gravitational pull of seeing our needs in a self-centered light! As strongly as we long for intimacy, it's amazing to discover that God wants it far more than we do. Even when sin first wedged itself between God and man, it was God who missed man (Genesis 3:8-10) while man hid.

Later in Israel's history, God's prophets stood in the path of a runaway nation intent on spending its lusts in idolatry and seeking its security in political alliances with pagan kingdoms. One of them named Hosea married, at God's direction, a woman who violated the intimacy and fidelity of their relationship with anyone crossing her path. Like God's heart toward us, Hosea rushed to buy the woman off the slave block after her repeated unfaithfulness left her nothing else.

In Jesus, God's aching heart for us to know Him blazes up like fire. His parable of the prodigal son (Luke 15:11-32) told of a heavenly Father's love that never quit yearning after a wayward son. He wept brokenheartedly over Jerusalem (Matthew 23:37; Luke 13:34), lamenting that God's people fled Him in pursuit of their own passions and pursuits (John 1:10,11; 3:19,20).

God's timeless longing for man can be traced not only in the tracks of His tears but in the outline of a cross. Crucifixion stood as certainly one of the most excruciating, diabolical ways that someone of that day could die. When the Romans wanted to crush the rebellious tendencies of their subjects, the public agonies of those nailed or lashed to crosses along highways and on hilltops worked very well. Death intimidates us all, even Christians who know doctrinally that it has no final power over us.

Why then Jesus' passionate focus on a death that anyone else would do anything to avoid? When Peter tried to dissuade Him from the cross, Jesus whirled and accused him of doing Satan's work (Matthew 16:21-23). Even as the disciples walked with Jesus along the road to Jerusalem for the last time, He pressed on ahead with a strange intensity that intimidated the rest (Mark 10:32). Although He knew what was coming, Jesus flew in the face of common sense and self-preservation and pressed on to the cross.

> While we were still helpless, at the right
> time Christ died for the ungodly. For one will

hardly die for a righteous man; though perhaps for the good man someone would dare even to die. But God demonstrates His own love toward us, in that while we were yet sinners, Christ died for us (Romans 5:6-8).

As the debris and clutter of every disappointing venture and relationship litters our insides, we may be tempted to plunge on alone either fueled by the drivenness of will or sputtering on the fumes of despair. But the subliminal ache of knowing and being known by God won't stop, won't lie still. Our heart was made to hear His voice. In the face of our failure, rebellion, and dread that no one exists who will brave and breach our defenses, God incredibly loves us, goes first in revealing His heart. And that heart longs for this intimacy far more than we do.

The Gift Nobody Wants

The visible trappings of truth stood in place but the erosion had been going on for years. Sometimes publicly through the spiritual bankruptcy of the king and more often in the privacy of every heart, decent and honest aspirations slipped their leash while wearing religious masks. The calendar, architecture, and furniture of faith were there. People knew the proper motions to make, the right answers to give. But a nation's soul had become a stranger to God who loved it.

Things really haven't changed. Our buildings, calendars, and furniture are well in place too. We too can give the right answers if asked because we know the religious vocabulary of the people of God.

But down deep in our lives, the cream of our lives is spent on the real things that spur us on: the career, the education, the money and what it can buy us—a hundred and one ventures of private concern. God is the One who is supposed to bless, provide, support, and protect us while we go after these. Jeremiah stood as judgment loomed like a crashing wave over God's people and said to them and to us:

> Thus says the Lord, "Let not a wise man boast of his wisdom, and let not the mighty man boast of his might, let not a rich man boast of his riches; but let him who boasts boast of this, that he understands and knows Me, that I am the Lord who exercises lovingkindness, justice, and righteousness on earth; for I delight in these things," declares the Lord (Jeremiah 9:23,24).

We will ask Him for everything but Himself. *But God Himself is the greatest gift He can bestow.* Jesus' words on this are incredible.

> He who has My commandments and keeps them, he it is who loves Me; and he who loves Me shall be loved by My Father, and I will love him, and will disclose Myself to him (John 14:21).

> If anyone loves Me, he will keep My word; and My Father will love him, and We will come to him, and make Our abode with him (John 14:23).

> No longer do I call you slaves, for the slave does not know what his master is doing; but I have called you friends, for all things that I have heard from My Father I have made known to you (John 15:15).

Treasures in Strange Shapes

Treasures come in strange shapes. If we could choose anything to bring as a treasure into the presence of God, what would it be? A blue denim cap made from cuttings of worn blue jeans is my first choice. When I first met my wife, she wore these caps to keep her long hair back. I can never hold that cap in my fingers without seeing that sassy twinkle in her eye that drew me to her and remembering a thousand and one shared moments that knitted us together. Should the opportunity arise, I would cast that blue denim cap before God's throne as the elders of Revelation cast their crowns.

Jesus offers us the treasure of His friendship. We can be rather callous in our relationships, taking them for granted and learning only by their loss what they meant. We can be consumptive, needy, and greedy as well, seeing our relationship as solely a matter of finding the right person to love us without weighing our investment in return. True friends are rare.

For reasons still a mystery to me, a college vice-president befriended me during my student days. We served on a board together and he would shoot at me under the table with his pipe while lawyers poring over legal briefs made long meetings even longer. His secretary held phone calls while we ate gumdrops in his office.

One night I crept into the back of a college symphony concert I promised to attend. Grimy from work I had just left, I hid in the darkness, figuring to duck out quickly. But I didn't realize it was almost intermission. The orchestra stopped. Lights right over my head came on and people thronged out the doors, trapping me in the glare. I didn't look very symphonic. Dr. Still walked back one aisle escorting his wife. When he saw me, he made a beeline to where I stood—mortified—and introduced his wife. While I stood mumbling apologetically, she unhesitatingly shook my grimy hand and said that Dr. Still had told her so much about me. She was glad we could finally meet.

Today an administration building stands on campus named after Dr. Dana Still. He certainly left his mark on the university. He marked me by extending the gift of friendship. I am an inch taller for the privilege.

Real friendships are always privileges—gifts and treasures upon which one has no claim but which are freely
offered. They breathe an ennobling dignity into the must-
iest corners of our lives. They lift our gaze and square our
shoulders. Friendships mean that the heart of another person has become home. Home is more than just a place of
residence; at home we can plod around in flip-flops and a
bathrobe, with our hair pointing off in more directions
than a compass face, and it's okay. We can slump in a chair,
prop up our feet, and let out a busy day with a long sigh.
Home is where our dreams and secrets are not only safe but
take root and grow into realities. At home we are valued,
cared for, and secure.

Jesus Christ offers His friendship, His heart, as home.
He does it without hesitation, knowing the worst about us.
It comes certainly undeserved. And it was definitely the
galvanizing point for the disciples. His friendship drew
them to Christ, welded their spirits to His, and broke them
in shame when they failed, deserted, and betrayed Him.
Scripture couches the friendship of Jesus in terms of the
most sacred intimacies.

> All things have been handed over to Me by
> My Father, and no one knows who the Son is
> except the Father, and who the Father is except
> the Son, and anyone to whom the Son wills to
> reveal Him (Luke 10:22).

Knowing the Father

What kind of intimacies pass between the first two
Persons of the Trinity? It seems intrusive, even blasphe-
mous, to try to imagine. No one really knows the Father
except the Son. I remember my father very well. He was a
steelworker, a crane operator in the assembly yard of a U.S.
Steel plant outside Pittsburgh. The men he worked with
knew him, too. Some feared him; all respected him. More
than one man owed his life to "Bub" Swartz. He told

supervisors and foremen what to do, and they did it! Dad said to me once, "David, when I throw the lever and lift 25 tons of steel into the air, I outrank the president of U.S. Steel." That wasn't bragging; he was telling the truth.

But all those welders, riveters, setup men, and hookup men who worked with him never knew him like I did. They saw him as a tough man who had to be respected, someone they would have no trouble with as long as they did their job. I saw him in ways they never would have imagined.

Dad was a man who gave me two incredible gifts. One was the gift of touch. Right up through the day I left home to be married, I knew his touch of affection in a variety of ways: a hug, a swat on the backside, an arm around my shoulder, a tousling of my hair. His hands were huge, but always tender.

Dad also gave me the gift of tears. The men at the mill thought my dad was tough. They wouldn't have recognized the man who sat and wept with me when my dog died, and who allowed me to cry with him when his dad died.

On the day of my wedding, both of Dad's gifts were intertwined. All through the ceremony, the two of us wept for joy. Regardless of what others thought, neither of us was embarrassed, because the tears were something shared between us.

Later that day, my bride and I went to the motel to change clothes. Dad and I hadn't had much opportunity to talk after the ceremony, so when he walked into the room, the response was spontaneous. A 23-year-old man raced across the room and leaped into the air. Dad caught me and held me up off the floor in a long hug. I can still feel the warmth of his body and the gentle strength of his arms. I can still smell his Old Spice and the minty aroma of the Tums he always carried. For all the time they spent with him, those steelworkers didn't know half the man that was there.

This intimacy isn't for everyone (see Luke 10:23,24). Do

we want it badly enough to be honest, vulnerable, and obedient? If so, we will discover that the richest intimacy humans can know—intimacy with God—will fit us like a personally tailored glove.

3

〰〰

A Contagion Worth Catching

Peeple who know God are a different cut from people who merely believe in Him. A number of things firm up like concrete in the lives of those intimate with God. One is that knowing God well eclipses all other external realities. God never promises Christians immunity from living under the same pressures that threaten to shred mind and spirit and crush the body of anyone else (John 17:15; 1 Corinthians 5:9,10).

But intimacy with God lays resiliency in our lives like brickwork. The tradition of early Christianity hints that the apostle Paul may not have been much to look at. If so, it's understandable. The hardships he endured, the persecution he suffered, and the constant mental stress of caring in absentia for churches he loved would be enough to prematurely age and batter the mind and body of anyone. In the middle of his ministry he wrote, "Therefore we do not lose heart, but though our outer man is decaying, yet our inner man is being renewed day by day" (2 Corinthians 4:16).

God strengthens us in spite of all the wearing down the world can dish out. I have a low tolerance for pain. Perhaps that explains why I can't stomach much of a pithy book written by a man named John Foxe over 400 years ago. He wrote his book to pay tribute to those who had suffered horribly and undeservedly for the gospel as well as to shame those who perpetrated these atrocities. *Foxe's Book of Martyrs* tells again and again of the greatest spiritual ecstasy, conviction, and courage in the face of cultural and psychological pressure that would snap the will of most people like a twig and pain that would reduce me to whimpering jelly.

Persecution does not necessarily make us stronger, but it does set the stage for those intimate with God to stand like oaks as monuments to the truth and power of the gospel. If people who were burned alive, blown up, cut in half, and starved could sing the praise of Jesus, He can certainly raise a fountain of joy and grace to erupt and bubble up through our heart in force and in the face of the opposition and hurdles we encounter. Sometimes God does not take the pressure off. Sometimes we're so fixated on asking for this that we fail to notice that what He really offers is more of Himself.

Strange Companions

Physical illness and pain are strange but frequent companions to those who genuinely know God. Their illness serves not to hobble them but almost to launch them into His presence—not for themselves, but to enjoy Him and to help heal others. Jesus said that the people who would be greatest in heaven would surprise us (Matthew 19:30).

I have a hunch I know one of these in advance. The joyous spirit that rises up to all who meet her hints nothing of the spinal pain that almost completely immobilizes her. She is an encouragement to everyone who encounters her, and I would drag myself across a Detroit expressway with my tongue at rush hour for her prayers. While she and her husband are far from rich, and physical pain and other hurts have dealt them cruel blows, she has gone deep with God and counts knowing Him as real wealth.

Being intimate with God overshadows not only the biting realities of persecution and suffering, but knowing Him overrides the press of daily externals as well. The apostle Paul never had a transmission go out on the expressway, but he knew the daily grind of existence of his day. As a tentmaker, he worked hard with his hands and trafficked in the marketplace merchandising his goods. He endured the backbiting and pettiness of people who claimed to be his brothers and sisters in Christ. Along with the stonings, imprisonments, and other hardships, Paul had to live with the daily aggravations and difficulties anyone might face. When he said, "I can do all things through Him who strengthens me" (Philippians 4:13), Paul included surviving the press of daily stuff right along with the rest.

Tom worked as a high-level technician with the phone company and earned over 80,000 dollars a year. Jesus Christ began to cause ferment deep inside Tom, which led him to serve in new ways. But his agitation of spirit intensified and became infectious. He and his wife both hungered for more from Christ. After much prayerful struggle, they walked away from Tom's attractive salary and their comfortable lifestyle to begin a new church in a rural mountain community.

Within a year they went from 80,000 dollars a year to 10,000. Tom and his wife live in a house they built themselves from salvaged materials. In the process of what many would see as real sacrifice, their lives have become cisterns from which the sweetness of Christ flows up from deep within to nourish all they meet. Even though they must occasionally dip into the church's food pantry for themselves, they wouldn't return to their old lives for twice the money Tom made before.

Forged Like Steel

Being intimate with God forges spirits of steel. John the Baptist became the chisel he was in God's hand after years of solitude with God. Later, as Peter and John backed the very leaders who conspired to murder Jesus Christ into a corner, the Jewish leaders noted they had been with Jesus (Acts 4:13). They weren't drawn by doctrine or philosophy. Theories of eschatology or epistemology don't make people embrace the flames at the stake or face lions in the arena without fear so that the torturers were converted witnessing the manner of their dying. Jesus said, "I, if I be lifted up from the earth, will draw all men to Myself" (John 12:32). *It's Jesus Christ Himself that draws.*

Yet because we crave blessing, healing, and protection, we will ask Him for everything but Himself. Jesus doesn't want to draw us to buildings, programs, or religious organizations. He wants to draw us to Himself—the closer the better. On their last evening together, John, the disciple Jesus loved, lay with his head on the Lord's chest (John 13:23). What must it have been like to be six inches from the face of God, to feel the rise and fall of every breath, to hear the voice that called the stars into being resonate from within the Lord's chest?

On vacations, I rarely divulge that I'm a pastor. It's not that I'm ashamed of what I do, but just that I find it easier to have honest conversations with people. One summer on a camping trip in Tennessee, I met a young couple from Ohio. As we talked, I learned many interesting things about them, including that they had been Christians for about two years. I asked how those two years had been. "No problem," they rifled back. "It's been great. One blessing after another, with every day better than the one before. Isn't that the way it's been for you?"

"No," I calmly replied, "it hasn't." For 24 years I've sputtered through erratic cycles of repentance, mediocrity, and faithfulness. For one period of almost three years I seethed hotly deep inside with rebellion and anger. My prayer life has had the consistency of a yo-yo. At 42, I'm subject to temptations I naively thought would never be a problem. I'm still falling over some of the same junk I brought with me into Christ.

Life hasn't gotten easier. It is rarely convenient, and obedience often feels like leaning into a cold prevailing wind. Sometimes the pressures of ministry makes me envious of the UPS deliveryman. But I can't get enough of Jesus. The richness of knowing Him still brings me running every time. In my spirit, seeing His face is life. No rebellion is worth holding, no idols worth clutching, no sin of attitude worth concealing, no pretenders for first place in my life worth entertaining at the expense of forfeiting His friendship and His touch.

As we yield to the cultural maladies of Western society, even we Christians too quickly look for healing and strength to techniques, therapies, scientific developments, and the never-ending output of technology. While these have their place, messiahs spun from the mind and hands of man can't reach through the darkness without and within. But in knowing Jesus, I discover the face and heart that undergirds and sustains the universe. And whether the path to Him was plowed through philosophical and spiritual quest or through hedonistic dissipation, we always learn, much to our surprise, that it was in fact He who sought us.

Treasuring Intimacy

We live in a tabloid society where fame has eclipsed greatness, where celebrities have currency while prophets do not. The right to gawk grips us even inside the church. But loving to spy into the vitals of lives, relationships, and things best left private soils us in heart and mind and callouses us toward much in the human situation that should inspire both awe and compassion.

Intimacy demands privacy. To air precious aspects of intimacy with God and others violates and cheapens them. Part of the real ugliness of pornography lies in its wrenching sexuality from a context of hidden intimacy and commitment and tossing it into the gutter to be gawked at by anyone. I am amazed at the things Scripture reveals to our eyes. The appearance of the burning bush to Moses and the accounts of his time with God on Mount Sinai are really none of our business. Abraham's struggle with the command to sacrifice Isaac is poignant. Reading of Mary's encounter with Jesus on Easter morning makes me feel I'm intruding on a sacred moment.

We know we've begun to treasure intimacy when we turn our head in the presence of the sacred and holy. To dignify, honor, and respect the intimacy that God has with others, I must renounce the urge to peer over the shoulder of others in their vulnerable moments before Him. When I preside over the table at the Lord's Supper or stand while others kneel at the prayer rail, I turn my eyes away as God ministers His grace. Some holy moments are violated by an audience.

Sometimes we do more than intrusively stare. To gossip is to be a pornographer in spirit. When we indiscriminately pass along things about others, we take things that usually should be treasured in prayer and throw them into the street. We pander the failings and foibles of others to get attention for ourselves. Gossip brutalizes both the one who gossips and the victim. To exaggerate fallen aspects of testimonies to impress the baser tastes of a Christian audience is pornographic. Our evil is not to be put under the glare of the spotlight (Ephesians 5:11,12).

Not all spiritual experiences are to be shared. The Hebrew word for knowing God is the same as the knowing of a husband and wife in sexual intimacy and union. While this may embarrass and rebuke our stony, arid, and sterile pantomimes of worship, it definitely means that not everything that happens between God and man is for public eyes. Among the postresurrection appearances of Jesus that Paul lists is one to Peter (1 Corinthians 15:5). Nowhere in Scripture do we get the details. Possibly, because of

Peter's denials, more than the encounter described in John 21:15-22 was needed. Peter could have spilled it all on a Christian TV talk show or broke the story with a bang at the Christian Booksellers Association international convention, but we may never know what happened.

As a young Christian, I knew a businessman who took a bunch of us under his wing. Mel loved Christ and had been powerfully used in ministry. All of us in our apartment just knew he must have had some incredible experiences with God, and we itched for a few spiritual "ghost" stories. When we pressed him, Mel just grinned, recognizing our childish immaturity. "God and I have had some tremendous times," Mel said tenderly. His eyes misted as he looked past us over a lifetime of wonderful memories. "But they're too personal to be shared." To pull out the pearls he treasured in his heart just to impress someone else would have cheapened and violated them.

Joy in the Arms of Fire

Richard Wurmbrand spent years of suffering and torture in a Romanian prison for the crime of preaching Christ. While his story tells of beatings, deprivation, and hardship, his life rings unmistakably of someone intimate with God. In a cell too cramped to permit lying down and always lit to prohibit sleep, Wurmbrand stood one night in nothing but rags and in pain from the latest beating. Ice caked the walls, There in the most fertile ground imaginable for self-pity, depression, and hatred to sprout, Richard Wurmbrand flourished. He reported being bathed in the strangest warmth. Scarred, weak, and torn in body and mind, he literally danced for joy.

Knowing God brings His wonderful light into every crevice and nuance of our habitual darkness. To say, really believing it, that I am utterly alone is to be stabbed through the heart with ice. We were made to know the voice of God over the roar of our days and to feel His touch on our tears in the dark of the night. Our selfish spurning of Christ's love only spurs Him to pursue us more intently.

To embrace God is risky. It means reaching out to embrace a pillar of fire and yet not be consumed. It means facing the lion only to be encircled by paws with claws folded in and to nestle deep into a mane as big as a feather bed. To embrace God in the face of Jesus Christ is risky and yet the greatest security of all, for He always embraces back, no matter who else may not.

4

Life in His Hand

Aman sitting at his kitchen table stares out across his backyard in the middle of the night. Steam rises from a cup of coffee that will go untouched and grow cold. He had plans and dreams just like anyone else. Maturity, skills honed to a sharp edge, and years of faithful service hadn't spared him this moment. They called it "early retirement" and it was supposed to be a favor. But now a mature man on the cutting edge of his profession feels forced out at a time of high productivity, only to be replaced by younger men with lower salaries. What would he do now?

Honest questions about meaning and purpose in life get lost in the surface rush and swirl of our lives. But sometimes they leak out at odd moments late at night or during that last hour when everyone is winding down at the office Christmas party.

Our idea of what life is all about and what makes it tick may sound impressive as we stand in circles sloshing punch in Styrofoam cups. But finding meaning in life that can carry the weight of living and survive the acid test of dying is a quest that will continue to rudely force itself upon us. Many people spend years thinking they have the key, only to watch it crumble to ashes in a cruel, unexpected moment. Others may think meaning and purpose a futile pursuit, and so spend their years and appetites on themselves. Some build houses without windows out of the few scraps that emptiness and despair leave, and then move in. Why am I here? I need more than the latest trendy ontology-of-the-month. I need an answer bigger than I am that smacks of truth—something that would hold even if the universe collapses.

The Glue of the Universe

Astronomers tell of reaching toward the outer fringes of known space with telescopes and instruments of incredible precision and sophistication. Men like Albert Einstein reached into the same years earlier without space technology and saw in their minds what others would later largely confirm. Einstein and later men such as Robert Jastrow sound that unmistakable note of awe in their writings of people who sense they touch infinity.

Coming to God as He has revealed Himself in the face of Jesus Christ, we do not touch infinity. We embrace the mind, the Person, that Einstein postulated was behind all reality in time and space. In Colossians Paul wrote:

> By Him all things were created, both in the heavens and on earth, visible and invisible, whether thrones or dominions or rulers or authorities—all things have been created by Him and for Him. And He is before all things, and in Him all things hold together (Colossians 1:16,17).

Both out in space, where quasars emit their intense radio waves and black holes swallow light as well as in the inner space of every atom, the sustaining force integrating and perpetuating it all is the power of the Person of Jesus Christ. Not His power but His very Being gives pulse to everything in time and space. Should all existence vaporize into nothing, Jesus Christ still stands unshakable and unchanging. Bound to Him by steel cords of faith and grace, our life can have meaning and purpose even when the only universe that's imploding is the one we carry in our heart.

Genetics of Spirit

Tim comes to the church door regularly for some sandwiches and milk. Homeless and street smart, Tim knows every warm corner and free handout in the area, so we see him about once a week. We never turn him away, for two reasons. One is that he is hungry. But one day Tim came not to ask for food. He asked if he could use our rest room. From somewhere he had scrounged a bar of soap, but none of the fast-food places or other of his haunts would allow him to use their washroom to clean himself up.

Tim's voice choked as he said, "Pastor, just because I'm on the street doesn't mean I have to smell like an animal. I have just enough money to get some new clothes at the resale shop, but I don't want to do that until I clean up. Can I use the sink in your rest room?" The second reason we never turn Tim away is that he and I have something in common. We both bear the thumbprint of God; we are both created in God's image.

We are all cast in the spiritual genetics of our Father, the living God; we are made in His image. On the surface that's not always apparent. We're so prone to attach value and meaning to appearances which can be superficial and misleading. Tim didn't look much like someone with God's nature squirreled away somewhere inside. Sometimes I don't either. Not only are appearances deceiving, but sin does a caustic work of stripping and peeling us of any sense of meaning beyond any transient concern.

An old house stood on a hill overlooking my hometown. We said it was haunted, and one night a friend and I crept in. During the depression the house had been owned by a wealthy family. What remained of the furnishings testified that the house must have been a showplace. I remember picking up canceled checks for thousands of dollars. Now the house remains—a looted, battered shell of something once beautiful. Much of the landscape within modern man smacks of decay and is littered with wreckage. But while that may be so, we are a wreck of something magnificent.

The first chapter of Genesis portrays man as the capstone of God's creative work. God saw that His work was "very good" (Genesis 1:31). Man stood as the pinnacle of that work. Scripture says repeatedly that God's signature and hand are evident throughout His creation (Romans 1:19,20). But just as only my son has my eyes or my daughter my nose, man uniquely reflects God's image. While this should undergird our lives with a deep sense of meaning and purpose, the value structure of the world around us puts us on the treadmill of its own standards, leaving us exhausted and empty.

The world we live in values performance and achievement. How we're doing defines who we are. Superiority in function overrides quality of being. Success in doing buys influence. Richness in a person often lies ignored. A garbageman's life simply doesn't compare in currency with that of a CEO. A world where success and achievement in every facet of life is the measure is a chilly and unforgiving place to live a very frail, fallible life. Losing or failing at our function shatters our meaning and purpose. We're no longer sure what we're about or why we're here. When those golden images have been dashed to crumbs, the marks of God's image in us are the hooks of meaning that won't give or break. They ground meaning and purpose in who I am instead of in what I do or accomplish.

Marks of God's Image

One mark of God's image is mind. God doesn't have hands; He is Spirit. Scripture references to the hands, feet, or eyes of God are called anthropomorphisms—symbolic representations to aid us in understanding. God's creative power and force lies in His mind. As He conceives in His mind, it takes on form in reality. Man, while less than God, has great power to think and create.

The sculptures of Michelangelo, the music of a nearly deaf Beethoven, and the architecture of Frank Lloyd Wright all point beyond the men to their maker. All that beauty and structure could never emanate from a mind that was nothing more than cosmic accident. Their kin are found in strange places. In big-city winters, the poor shuffle from public building to public building trying to stay warm. Fast-food places let them stay as long as they have at least a cup of coffee to nurse. Public libraries and Christian Science reading rooms let you stay as long as the doors are open and you behave.

It's strange to see hands in fingerless gloves peruse the *Wall Street Journal*, the *New York Times*, or even the *Manchester Guardian*. I've had incredible conversations on Shakespeare, world politics, and history with people bundled up in thrift shop coats. The poor have time to read and think when they're not scraping to survive. And many do think. Their flexing of the muscles of thought evokes my respect and cloaks them with one of the few dignities that has not eluded them. As Scripture enjoins us to love God with all our mind (Luke 10:27), we wrap ourselves in the same dignity as we flex the same muscles of thought.

The exercise of will and depth of emotion both stand as two more witnesses to God's genetics in our life. The behavior patterns of animals are instinctive. They respond without giving much if any conscious thought. Salmon swim upstream to spawn out of instinct. It is ridiculous to expect a salamander to exercise moral judgment pertaining to right and wrong or to do other than what salamanders have done for thousands of years.

But man has the powerful capacity of will. He can choose to be like others or to act very differently. We make decisions as to career choices, marriage partners, or relational patterns that are not programmed responses to inbred stimuli and that powerfully impact our lives. Not only to choose, but to choose morally, bears testimony to the mark of God's chisel on us. Living in a twilight of values, with most people no longer believing in absolutes, we strangely still appeal to a common right or consensus of value. Even if we no longer agree on what is right, it's still right to do right and to feel outrage at wrong.

The moral response of people who don't go to church or evidence any belief in God whatsoever betrays His thumbprint. In our northern winters, those unemployed or otherwise on limited incomes can't always afford to maintain their home heating systems. It's not uncommon for a house to occasionally explode from a gas leak. Many times, but not always, the family isn't home. The neighborhood response to these blown-out families is always incredible— the outrage, the grieving, the spontaneous generosity otherwise unseen. Food, clothes, furniture, household articles, even entire homes given without reserve by those who barely had enough for themselves smacks of the touch of Someone outside us. The exercise of will and power to make moral choices, although sin can blind and paralyze both with devastating consequences, dignify our lives with a dignity reflecting the face of God our Creator and Sustainer.

The Bible uses strong language describing our sinful nature. But even when words like "wicked" and "evil" come into play, Scripture never attacks the personhood of people created in the image of God. The tragedy is that man is in bondage to a terrible nature he is powerless to throw off—a nature that produces wickedness and evil in spite of our good resolve and intentions (Romans 7:13-25).

Created and Bought

If we have meaning in life because we are created in the image of God, that meaning multiplies a hundredfold in light of the cross of Jesus Christ. Salvation describes not only the healing of the otherwise irretrievably shattered image of God but also its transformation into the image of His Son (Romans 8:29). The cross stands as a constant reminder of our worth to God; it was the price He was willing to pay.

> While we were still helpless, at the right time Christ died for the ungodly. For one will hardly die for a righteous man; though perhaps for the good man someone would dare even to die. But God demonstrates His own love toward us, in that while we were yet sinners, Christ died for us (Romans 5:6-8).

The tough nuts of theology that we have difficulty cracking can really help us if we refuse to sidestep them. Paul wrote in Ephesians 1:4,5, "He chose us in Him before the foundation of the world, that we should be holy and blameless before Him. In love He predestined us to adoption as sons through Jesus Christ to Himself, according to the kind intention of His will."

Election points to God's free sovereignty in choosing us. Every child knows about being chosen, and almost all know the pain of being chosen last. Whether it's a pickup game on the playground or a spelling bee in school, the process is the same. The captains start with the best and the most popular. Some yet to be chosen jump up and down, waving their hands, while others plead and beg. Some just stare at the ground. But by the time the picking is done, every kid in the group knows exactly what he's worth in his peer group. The last one chosen really isn't chosen at all; he just meanders over to the group that is stuck with him.

But one day it was different for me. In high school gym class we divided up for basketball. "Mac," a guy I respected, was one of the captains. Plenty of players better than I were still standing when I heard him call my name. Mac picked me! We weren't close friends; in fact I thought he never knew I was around. But two things happened: First, I grew six inches in sixty seconds, and second, I played far and away the best basketball game of my life.

Election and predestination mean that God chose me. I had neither claim on Him nor anything to offer. He didn't care how well I could shoot, hit, or spell. Ultimately we will never understand love as long as we insist on a reason for its existence. As long as we love or are loved because of an intrinsic quality or level of performance, what happens when the quality is lost or the performance cannot be sustained?

The Bible describes God's love in great depth but never explains it. Scripture does not require us to dissect it but to accept it, to revel in it and ground our lives upon it. God chose me not at the beginning of the game but before there was a game, before the foundation of the world. That He did this open-eyed, knowing far more intimately than I the depth of my failures and weaknesses, tells of His confidence not in me but in the power of the cross to be unleashed in my life.

No Mere Game

When God chooses us, it's not for a mere game but to be His. His end in view is that we should be His children. He "predestined us to adoption as sons." Adopted children sometimes struggle with feelings of rejection and anger over the idea of a parent who, for whatever reason, abandoned them. But hopefully they feel to a much greater degree the life-enriching reality of being wanted by someone else. Jesus Himself promised that His followers would not be left as orphans (John 14:18). Paul made the point more forcefully:

> You have not received a spirit of slavery
> leading to fear again, but you have received a
> spirit of adoption as sons by which we cry out,
> "Abba! Father!" The Spirit Himself bears wit-
> ness with our spirit that we are children of
> God, and if children, heirs also, heirs of God
> and fellow heirs with Christ, if indeed we suf-
> fer with Him in order that we may also be
> glorified with Him (Romans 8:15-17).

"Abba" is an intimate family name. Every morning I see parents pulling up to the curb and stopping long enough to get a quick kiss before rushing off to work. But when I dropped our two children off for kindergarten, we had more important things to do—we had a game to play. We always parked a short distance down the street from the school, where, after a hug and a kiss, my two children would take a few steps toward school. Every two or three steps they would stop and turn as if to see if I was still there. Then they would grin, wave, and say, "'Bye, Daddy!" I would grin and wave back. It really gave them a kick to see how many times they could get Dad to wave. We averaged about 20 waves a day.

What they never guessed was that every morning I looked years ahead to when they would one day walk away and be gone. I would have stayed for every "Daddy" they wanted to call out. I stood in the fall sunshine, the early spring rain, and the wind chills way below zero just to hear it one more time.

"Daddy." The sound of it vaporizes my lousiest day and brings me back to what's important like few things can. God has put it in the heart of every Christian to call out "Abba" a hundred times a day if he likes. He hears and treasures each utterance—one from the surgical waiting room, one over a checkbook whose balance is dwarfed by a mountain of bills, one from a tearstained pillow. For God to hear my "Abba" brings Him joy. For me to say it frames my life with meaning.

Embracing God

Passport from Heaven

Ambassadors, diplomats, and other public officials enjoy prestige and privilege. So do international business representatives globe-trotting from Frankfurt to London to Singapore. First-class accommodations in lodging, travel, and meals are standard fare. But there's a price for this. Nations and businesses only want the best representing them—the sharpest, the most experienced, the most educated. No political, military, or economic enterprise ever carried out by man can eclipse the kingdom of God. The advancement of God's kingdom is the one supreme venture undergirding or superseding all other concerns of mankind. If this is so, what kind of people does God choose to represent Him?

> Consider your calling, brethren, that there were not many wise according to the flesh, not many mighty, not many noble; but God has chosen the foolish things of the world to shame the wise, and God has chosen the weak things of the world to shame the things which are strong (1 Corinthians 1:26,27).

> We have this treasure in earthen vessels, that the surpassing greatness of the power may be of God and not from ourselves (2 Corinthians 4:7).

If you were launching the most important venture in world history, would you start with the people Jesus chose? He started with earthen vessels—people of common clay, forged of the common, ordinary, and breakable stuff of life. The lives that populate church history and fill heaven stand as castaways and rejects, the passed-over and ignorable. Only the lens of historical distance makes them loom large. A closer look reveals Someone living through stubble and straw lives, using them to blaze eternal marks in history.

Our celebrity-obsessed society with all its glitz and hair-spray has infected the church. The people who look good on stage or in front of the cameras are the authorities, experts, and models. But worldly limelight and clout do not authenticate the credentials of those whom God would have represent Him in the world.

Fit for the Jewels

A museum housed a display of priceless jewels. The glass had been carefully polished and the black velvet deftly arranged just right, with spotlights trained at the best angle to feature the jewels. We, along with many others, viewed the display. People heaped praise on the jewels; nobody gawked at the display case. Nobody said, "Wow! Did you ever see a display case like this? Margaret, give your camera to that guy and come over here so we can get a picture." God is looking for ordinary lives who will allow *Jesus Christ* full display. He looks for them in every walk and station of life, every culture. Sometimes the outside must be sanded and the inside scrubbed, but He will settle for nothing less than something fit to display His Son.

A well-made cabinet is almost invisible, so aptly does it enhance its display. But a nicked-up one, with scratched and dirty glass, usually cheapens what it holds in the eye of the beholder regardless of its real value. God builds with scraps, the things in which people see no purpose and meaning. His tools include blood and grace. His work is sure and complete. When God is finished, the case will not only fittingly display the jewel, but the case itself will strangely resemble the jewel!

5

Seeing the
Unseen

L ast birthday I received a small shortwave radio. Now I'm only a button and a dial away from the BBC in London, Radio Havana, or Radio Cairo. But as I listen through the crackling static, my imagination goes out over the airwaves to nations and cultures I can touch no other way. There's something riveting about being taken in our mind beyond our experiences, limitations, and failures. Stretched that far just once, we never snap back to the size we once were.

When I was 11, I joined the band and started learning to play the tuba. Since tubas don't play much melody, my practicing in our basement consisted mostly of assorted "oomphs," blats, and belching sounds that sounded more like severe plumbing and sewage problems than music. But the day of my first group practice came and I sat in a room with a hundred other musicians. The downbeat fell as I took a deep breath and blew. For the first time I heard how my sounds knitted together with other sounds to make ensemble music. My life would never be the same. I felt buoyed up as if on the edge of a great wave.

Jesus had a special knack of enticing those He encountered with the eternal, the unseen, and the unimaginable. We tend to be monolithic in our evangelism, locked into one or two memorized methods. But Jesus approached people as individuals. His words rebirthed hope long thought dead and gave birth to hope never imagined.

Jesus sparked new meaning and purpose in life by enticing people with new identities. He saw something special, for example, in Simon Peter. We judge by appearance and performance, but Jesus always sees what grace can mine from the heart. Peter had probably never been easy to be around. In the Gospels we see him quick to speak, boisterous, and hot-tempered, mercurial in temperament and full of himself. At their first meeting Jesus said to him, "You are Simon the son of John; you shall be called Cephas (which translated means Peter)" (John 1:42).

Peter, which means "rock" in Greek, knew of his shortcomings. Aren't we sometimes painfully aware of ours? But Jesus said, "I will make you a rock." He makes us what we could never make ourselves. He produced a stability in Peter that was unshakable, something that the whole early church could lean on if need be. Peter may have cowered and denied Christ at the question of a young girl, but he stood undaunted and bold in the faces of the Jewish officials who conspired to murder Jesus (Acts 4:1-22).

What's in a Name?

For us, a name isn't much more than a label, an ID tag of sorts. But for people living in biblical times and cultures, a name described the character and essence of its bearer. Once God transforms a heart, the old name no longer fits and must be changed. Abram became Abraham, meaning "father of a multitude" (Genesis 17:5)—a living reminder of God's promises. Jacob, a conniving "supplanter," became Israel, "the one who prevails with God." In Jesus Christ we find both the labels given by others and those earned by our flawed, sinful living peeled away.

A girl I knew from kindergarten up through high school got pushed to the side by her peers in adolescence. She was smart and outgoing and came from a fine family. But for some reason she never fit the ever-changing early adolescent opinions of what's popular. She was ridiculed by many. To my knowledge, she never had a date of any kind. Even her name became a joke of sorts. I can't imagine how much pain she had choked down over those six years or so.

The summer after my first year of college I ran into a fellow high school graduate and we caught up on news. She challenged me to guess who was one of the most popular girls on campus. It was Sue. She had gotten a fresh start where all the old labels and images had been left behind. Now she could have a different life, where all that stored-up pain and scarring could be cleaned out. That's what Jesus did for Peter and can do for us. The labels that keep us padlocked in our shortcomings and failures are engraved too deeply in our spirit for us to peel off. But the power of Christ's forgiveness from the cross scours us of sin's liabilities so that what only God can conceive becomes reality. Jesus Christ desires no less for us than He did for Peter. As part of His letters to the churches in Asia Minor, Jesus says:

> He who has an ear, let him hear what the Spirit says to the churches. To him who overcomes, to him I will give some of the hidden manna, and I will give him a white stone, and a new name written on the stone which no one knows but he who receives it (Revelation 2:17).

The final effect of Christ's redemption on every facet of our lives will be so revolutionary and so stunning that nothing, not even the best, of this earthly life can describe or define it—certainly none of the labels that sin and our own self-condemnation grind into us. Conversely, the highest praise of men as well as our own best self-assessments will fade like morning fog in noonday sun in comparison to the finished work of Christ in us. It will take a new name to describe it, and Jesus Himself will give it to us. He has no intention of waiting until then, however, to start.

Another aspect of Jesus' infusing lives with meaning and purpose was His enticing men and women with new possibilities. In His drawing of Peter, Andrew, and Nathaniel, Jesus promised to bring out of their experience the unexpected and the unforeseen.

> He said to them, "Follow Me, and I will make you fishers of men" (Matthew 4:19).

> Jesus answered and said to him, "Because I said to you that I saw you under the fig tree, do you believe? You shall see greater things than these." And He said to him, "Truly, truly, I say to you, you shall see the heavens opened, and the angels of God ascending and descending on the Son of Man" (John 1:50,51).

Unimagined Heights

The one who follows Jesus faithfully will find himself seeing and doing things he never would have imagined. None of the people in biblical or church history set out to make themselves what they became in God's hands. Abraham, Elisha, David, Isaiah, the apostles, and Paul all had their lives in motion in other directions. Only Moses made an attempt to be what God intended, but in his own strength—and he failed. When Jesus Christ works out new possibilities, He works in two ways: a new task and the degree of influence.

Jesus promised that Peter would become a fisher of men. The more we yield to Christ's work, the more we will find ourselves doing things we never would have imagined. We recently spent a weekend in Chicago with a group of Christians ministering there. They started over 20 years ago as a bunch of drifting hippies stranded in Chicago with a broken-down bus. Now over 500 of them live out of a common purse and base their ministry in a renovated hotel. They reach out to every spiritual and material need imaginable in a major city. They make gifted contributions in every facet of the arts, and they network with churches of every denomination and social service agencies, not only in their own city but around the world. Interns from Bible colleges come to learn from street-schooled people leading penetrating and innovative ministries.

I remember the Christians I knew in college over 20 years ago. God has taken us in amazing directions. Had someone told me I would be a pastor and writer, not only I but others would have laughed. But God has done what He has done.

A missionary's arrival on the field coincided with the onset of monsoon season. Primed with fresh zeal and full of self-confidence, the man and his wife sat and watched it rain for over a month. Restlessness and then depression set in. Here he came, cocked like a loaded pistol, with all his education and training, ready to make his mark for Christ. And now they sat cooling their heels watching the monsoon rains fall day after day.

One afternoon the man sat morosely watching it rain. He brooded and groused in his heart, feeling sorry for himself that such a great treasure for God as he was being wasted. Our pride rarely lets us carry such an attitude so transparently, yet buried in carefully done camouflage, many of us know this same feeling. That afternoon God spoke surely and quietly to his heart by saying, "It's your part to go deeper with Me. It's My part to spread you around."

Where Christ will spread the influence of one life given to Him we cannot imagine. Eugene Peterson has wisely said, "There is an enormous gap between what we think we can do and what God calls us to do. Our ideas of what we can do or want to do are trivial; God's ideas for us are grand."[3]

Richer Satisfactions

Jesus Christ also infuses lives with meaning and purpose by enticing us with new and richer satisfactions. Sometimes the things we most deeply want are lost most easily by pursuit—things like happiness, joy, fulfillment. The harder we strive the more they elude us.

Our society bristles with the lust for fulfillment more now than at any other time in our history. While we have always followed the bent of our sinful self-centeredness, it is now not only acceptable but fashionably desirable to pursue "something I just need to do" no matter how detrimental the effect on major adult responsibilities. Of course it's not wrong to want satisfaction or to feel fulfilled, but to be *consumed* even by a legitimate desire crosses over into idolatry.

In reality, the hungers of the heart we most long to satisfy can't really be filled until we stop looking into ourselves and become swallowed up in pursuit of something bigger than we are. Jesus said that all these things could be found by finding Him.

> The thief comes only to steal, and kill, and destroy; I came that they might have life, and might have it abundantly (John 10:10).

> He who has found his life shall lose it, and he who has lost his life for My sake shall find it (Matthew 10:39).

Jesus held out this promise to a Samaritan woman He met one day at a well (John 4:1-42). As she approached, Jesus asked her for a drink. Surprised that, both as a man and a Jew, He would speak to her, she lowered her defenses. Jesus said, "If you knew the gift of God, and who it is who says to you, 'Give Me a drink,' you would have asked Him, and He would have given you living water" (John 4:10).

At first all the woman heard was that Jesus could save her the hassle and chore of these daily trips to the well. What a tragic mistake we make in coming to Jesus only to see what He can do for us or how He can make our lives easier! His agenda runs far deeper and often finds us preoccupied at best, if not downright disinterested. Jesus took aim at the yearnings deep in this woman's heart, knowing that she was thirstier than she knew. But He would show her by asking about her husband.

When she replied that she had none, Jesus delicately but surgically pinpointed her vulnerability by saying He knew about her five earlier husbands as well as her current live-in situation. Possibly she had been widowed five times, but it's more likely there was a mix of deaths and divorces. Divorce was rather casual at the time, and the woman had little protection in what was a male-dominated society. Although living together without marriage no longer raises an eyebrow today, and people have always done it, it was still enough of a scandal in that society (especially in a small town) for her to be the object of gossip and public censure.

Could she have known the pain of bereavement? It's real and it lingers. A woman whose husband had been dead for two years asked me if I thought she was crazy because she kept her husband's pillow on the bed. The scent of her late husband's cologne was still on it.

How about the pain of a possible divorce? Nobody gets married hoping it will fail. Sometimes we marry the wrong people. Divorce, no matter how amiable, always brings cruel feelings of rejection. And because divorce was so casual in Jesus' day, a woman could be put out in the street and disgraced on the slightest pretense. What kind of rejection had she suffered at the hands of the wrong men that she would expose herself to the gossip and social ostracizing of the village? (Women usually came for water at the beginning of the day, and here it was noon. Was it in order to avoid the other women of the village?)

Maybe she had despaired of ever getting from any man the kind of love and commitment a real marriage takes and yet could not cope with the loneliness that would come to roost every night like a bird of prey. Maybe she felt the crush of having no other family to go to, and this was more of a relationship of survival. Cohabitants pooling their Social Security checks in order to make ends meet know how physical need can boil down the strongest values to one last element: to survive no matter what.

Whatever the situation, Jesus knew of her sin without whipping her with the word. She knew it too, if her speedy change of the subject to more spiritual matters means anything (John 4:19,20). Sin in every form is the attempt to fulfill a basic God-ordained need or desire gone awry because of our rebellion against God Himself. Trying to mine fulfillment from our bodies, minds, relational capacities, or glands while failing to see or wanting to admit that these things can only come when we're reconciled to God is not only futile but breeds crippling disillusionment.

Freeze-Framing the Outward

We might have seen the woman as most people of her day did. Seeing only part of anyone, we tend to "freeze frame" him or her, taking what we see and absolutizing it as if that were the entire person. That person at work who drives us crazy has sides of his or her personality that we've never seen. But what we see is what bugs us. Every human being is a person of vast inner space. Since God, man's Creator, is infinite, we should expect man's spirit to reflect largeness in its depth.

That's how Jesus saw the Samaritan woman. Townspeople saw a scandalous woman, Jews saw a Samaritan half-breed. Jesus, being God, saw her as she took shape in her mother's womb (Psalm 139:13). He never missed a moment of her growing up, witnessing every joy and pain

(Psalm 139:1-5). He winced over the grieving or rejection etched on her with the demise of each marriage. He grieved most of all at how she was straining with all her sinful nature could muster for what He alone could give. And Jesus was not about to let this lady's religious veneer get in the way now that she was so close.

Jesus knew of her real thirsts and of her sin-corroded attempts to meet them—thirsts for intimacy, thirsts to be loved unconditionally, thirsts to know God. The words of Jesus triggered something deep inside her like a key in a lock long rusted shut. So it is for all of us who find that knowing Jesus Christ taps into richer, deeper satisfactions than our abortive sin-plagued living without Him can provide.

The final dimension of Jesus' touch of significance in bringing meaning and purpose to human lives is the infusing of new dignity. Zaccheus (Luke 19:1-10) was a tax collector. The Romans used Jews to collect the taxes from their people. Because the Jews hated the Romans, the tax collectors were seen as traitors, and it wasn't uncommon to see them assaulted. Zaccheus' shortness, and the slights he suffered throughout his life because of it, possibly piled up a large backlog of hurt.

Zaccheus' diminutive body may have towered over his beaten-down spirit. He climbed up a tree to see over the crowd that blocked his view. Public officials in my city don't behave this way. A petty little dignity, the kind we bestow on ourselves, came with his title. But he left it at the base of the tree. We too must leave behind our passing attempts to clothe spiritual need and nakedness with scraps of pride if we will see Jesus Christ.

And Jesus saw him. Not only did Jesus see him, but He insisted on staying with him. At Jesus' words, Zaccheus grew six inches. Zaccheus promised half his goods to the poor and to make fourfold restitution to those he had cheated. His purse strings had been loosened by the dignity of grace. Jesus, with His eye on the depths of every heart, said that salvation had come to Zaccheus' house. A man looked down on by most others grew in spirit graced by a new dignity.

Jesus does the same for the obscure. While we may not be the object of ridicule or attack as Zaccheus may have been, millions of us live lives we feel would echo in a thimble—lives that are small and empty. Most of us know the Christmas story well enough to be at least passingly familiar with the angels and shepherds. In their day, shepherds weren't held in high esteem. In some eyes, being a shepherd was a step above begging. The only time many people thought about shepherds at all was when meat and wool became scarce in the market. They lived obscure lives unknown and unremembered. But then there came that night—the one whose light they would carry in their minds' eye the rest of their lives. The sky exploded with angels singing praise to God and announcing the birth of the Savior, Christ the Lord.

When we have good news, don't we want to tell someone? The better the news, the more urgent the need to tell. God had the most incredible news ever to break on mankind. He could have chosen anyone to be the first to hear. But God bypassed the important people, the power brokers, for the ignored and forgotten. After the shepherds had seen Jesus and broadcast the news through the town, they returned to the hills and the sheep. Regardless of how people may have looked at them from then on, God poured enough grace and glory into their lives that night to dignify the rest of their days.

Who Masters You?

Why does much of the meaning and purpose that Jesus Christ can bring to life seem lost in the lives of those who know Him? We must decode our ambitions and take hard looks at what drives and motivates us. The almost demonic pace of living that is exhausting so many people leaves little energy to probe the "whys" of what we do. It takes a marriage disintegrating, a rebellious child exploding, a career imploding, or our sanity cracking before some of us make ourselves examine what's going on. Jesus said, "No one can serve two masters" (Matthew 6:24). Jesus knew that, while no one can serve two masters, everyone surely has one master.

Who or what masters us? There may be no greater question we grapple with at any given time. As our lives grow and change over time, this question is never answered once for all but must be faced repeatedly. Many people launch into adult life out of a vacuum left when a parent or other important adult failed or abused them. Anger and unfulfilled attempts to get love or approval can sabotage lives later if these problems are not identified and resolved. Sometimes we're just selfish. Education, along with hard work and its rewards, can be nothing more than rungs on the ladder of our wants.

Who or what is really God in our lives? Our abstract beliefs aside, "god" is whatever we are pouring out the wine of the vitality of our lives for. Jesus saw that at heart, people spent the substance of their lives and gave first place to things that ruined them—sometimes during their temporal lives, but certainly in eternity. He knew the problem to be one of being mastered not so much by *bad* things as by *wrong* things. That's why Jesus replied to the rich young ruler as He did, when many of us would have seen nothing more than a fine young man who (along with his checkbook) would have made a fine church member (Matthew 19:16-22). Good, respectable things come to hold a degree of importance that only God should have. We cannot embrace God while holding on to anything else.

Four Clues

Four keys give some practical help for hungry or searching people. A little introspection in some seldom-examined areas could save us years of feeling that our faith is cheating us. First, what are our dreams? In unguarded free moments, where does our imagination run? Jesus said, "Where your treasure is, there will your heart be also" (Matthew 6:21). Our dreams stake out at least where we would like our treasure to be, if not where it really is. But whatever has genuinely captured us will be the stuff of our dreams and fantasies.

Our plans mark a second road to our treasure. When we go beyond dreaming to taking steps and making projections as to how these dreams can happen, we may be charting the course toward our treasure. Most of us dream and plan for a wide variety of short- and long-term ventures, both personal and professional. These hardly qualify as idolatrous usurpers of God's rightful place in our lives. But the things that own us, our treasure, always prod us beyond the daydreaming stage to action refusing to be denied.

How do we handle change? It's not usually a problem in things we don't care about. But change at a deep level, either for better or worse, is something we tolerate for that ultimate goal in our life. Our treasure will shape us, change us. Even if we don't like what the change may produce in our personalities, values, or relationships, it can be written off and absorbed as a price of the treasure. While this isn't always a conscious or reasoned decision, it always happens.

Where we invest dreams, plans, and a willingness to embrace change at a deep level, we must be careful. These are the concerns that can seduce us from what we say and know should be important. These are the concerns that can cause people who know God in Christ to play games, be phonies, and lie to themselves while the surface things all look fine. When God is the center and source of these, the heart is like the wick of a candle trimmed and waiting for the flame of God. When these three lie rooted in our sinful self-centeredness, we may be building our lives on the city limits of idolatry and spiritual adultery.

Sacrifice is one of the noblest gestures of which man is capable. It also can be the most powerful tool that our sinful nature can muster. It is the fourth quadrant we must examine. The desire for comfort, ease, and convenience runs so deep in everyone that where we deny ourselves these says something profound about us. The indictment against many of us, Christians included, is that the great sacrifices of our lives lie in the area of our own personal concern.

If we save money, cut down on vacation, and eat beans twice a week, we should be able to put that deck on the back of the house. If we remortgage the cottage and maybe take an extra job on weekends, we should be able to scrape together enough for Junior's first year at college.

Decks and college educations aren't the issue. If Jesus Christ means all we like to say He does, where is sacrifice like this in our lives for the kingdom of God? Our treasure always demands sacrifice. If we claim that something is the most important thing in life and yet have made no sacrifice for it, we're just deluding ourselves.

Where the four lines of dreams, plans, change, and sacrifice intersect, that is the functional "god" of our lives. That is our treasure and therefore where our heart is. That is our one master. We may not like what this says, but Jesus Christ is doing us a favor by walking through these areas showing us that we may not be the person we would like to think, or that our love for Him is not nearly as strong as our own self-centeredness. We will never know much of the love of Christ if we don't stop clutching things to our breast that we should drop. We'll never be free to embrace God until we do.

Escaping the Clay

People today resound with the emptiness of being full of the wrong things—full of themselves, full of the bankrupt promises of the world, full of destructive emotional baggage cherished too long to be jettisoned easily now. Jesus Christ makes no promises outside Himself. But in coming to Him with open arms we will find every promise of meaning and purpose fulfilled beyond our wildest imagination. New identities, possibilities, and dignities spring from His grace like spring perennials coming up through the snow.

General Montgomery, the great British general of World War II, wrote a book after the war on leadership and included a chapter about his boss, Winston Churchill. Commenting on how one man's fire carried England through the hard days of war, Montgomery said of him, "There was a certain magnificence about him which transformed the lead of other men into gold."[4]

Where Churchill evoked gold, Jesus evokes platinum. He infuses multidimensional life into the dreary days of empty people—people so desperate for meaning and purpose that they will drop everything they have foolishly clutched up till now that kept them from embracing Him.

6

⚮

Mercy in My Mess

On most Monday mornings I face 40 or so preschoolers. Our day-care center has chapel services which I'm glad to do, since those ten minutes are the only church which some of those kids ever get. Some come from broken or troubled families. For any number of reasons, many have no father present. That's why they listen so eagerly to me. It's not that my children's sermons are so great; it's just that I'm the most significant male figure some of them see all week. Whatever I use for an object lesson, they assure me they've got one. I could hold up a live walrus and someone would say, "Pastor Dave, I have one of those at home."

Of course, they don't really want to impress me with all they have. All they really want is my attention. One morning at the close of chapel I was talking with one of the workers when I felt a yank on my pant leg. I looked down into an urgent little face. "Pastor Dave," he began.

"Yes, son."

"Pastor Dave, your barn door is open," said the boy.

I stood there frozen at the thought that I had just been standing in front of almost 50 people. But then I knew these kids loved a good joke. After all, one little girl had stopped me in the hall on April Fool's Day and said, "Pastor Dave, Godzilla is right behind you!"

Leaning closer to the boy, I lowered my voice, asking, "Is it really?" He just nodded and gave a big sigh so much as to say, "Yep, Pastor Dave, you're dead."

Everybody has "barn door" moments. While some are nothing more than fleeting embarrassing occurrences, some are much more. Every human being has times when his or her failures, weaknesses, and sin become painfully evident both to themselves and to others. These times carve us deeply, right to the marrow of our bones. They can scar us for life or force us in new directions that make it possible for real life to go on.

But we need to remember that the worst enemy to any sense of intimacy, meaning, and purpose in life lives right inside our shirt collar. We spend much energy avoiding "barn door" moments or trying to conceal them once they occur. But some of the best time we can spend is to analyze not only how our "barn door" moments came to be but what they've done to us. While Jesus Christ brings to life all the wonderful things we've mentioned up to this point, not much will happen if we refuse to deal with these embarrassing moments in our past so that we don't have them sitting like bombs out in our future.

Cross Section of a Heartache

Paul wrote brilliantly to the Ephesian church. It's difficult to find six chapters as broad in scope as his letter to them. After writing grandly on God's greatness, Paul reminds them of their past as well.

You were dead in your trespasses and sins,
in which you formerly walked according to the

course of this world, according to the prince of the power of the air, of the spirit that is now working in the sons of disobedience. Among them we too all formerly lived in the lusts of our flesh, indulging the desires of the flesh and of the mind, and were by nature children of wrath, even as the rest (Ephesians 2:1-3).

Paul writes that they were "dead in trespasses and sins." Death, in Scripture, isn't the absence of pulse and respiration. "Dead" means that man's spirit is deliberately and defiantly unresponsive to God. We have cut ourselves off from God. The alienation and estrangement is on our part. Spiritual death is irreversible if all we have is our own strength.

In Romans 5:6 Paul says, "While we were still helpless . . ." To feel helpless is a crippler that comes in many shapes. And it currently is one of the most powerful levelers of people in Western society. We Americans deeply believe that hard work, education, science, and technology can solve anything, alleviate any problem. If we can put our hands on it or our minds at it we can fix anything. That's why helplessness is so devastating. Helplessness is reality punching us in the solar plexus saying, "There's nothing you can do about this." It shreds our cocky self-sufficiency and sandpapers our pride.

Sometimes externals do this. One man, looking back at how the collapse of his career almost ruined his life, wrote:

> I came back to reality . . . the reality that no matter how meticulously you plan your life, no matter how diligently you pursue your goals, no matter how many hours you work, no matter how dedicated you are, the bottom line is you just don't have total control over your life.[5]

Sometimes helplessness crushes us with a wave of broken health. Chronic severe pain can break down the components of someone's personality and spirit to mush. Sufferers of epilepsy and biochemical mental illness know that horrible feeling of being at the mercy of their body. Cancer patients know the "violated" feeling of having something dark growing inside them.

Helplessness can paralyze us. But it yields a mineload of wisdom if we'll listen. For one thing, it reminds us that we are not God. All of us tend to live lives of inflated boundaries; we are not all the person we would like to believe. Our limitations are often more serious and severe than we're willing to accept. We deeply resent others telling us what to do because nobody (including and especially God) can tell me how to run my life. Helplessness in my "barn door" times is a blessing because it strips me of pretense. The real me, the one I don't like and try to suppress, comes out. Not only am I a person who can't touch the stars, but I often lack the courage to reach across the table to those I love. Helplessness pounds the pride, that strangling and arrogant self-sufficiency, out of us. In fact, this is usually the only way the pride that padlocks us in death comes out.

Jacob had been a conniver all his life. Today deception and manipulation are a way of life for many families. In some societies, lying and stealing are virtues. Apparently Jacob's mother hatched the pathetic plot to deceive his age-ravaged father so that Jacob, her favorite, would receive the choice blessing (Genesis 27). Jacob's uncle Laban pulled a last-minute switch on Jacob's wedding night, giving his oldest daughter, Leah, instead of Rachel (Genesis 29:15-30).

But Jacob surpassed them both, taking to deception like an eagle to mountain air. Jacob trusted his shrewdness to make things happen in his life even after God had revealed Himself in a dream. He manipulated his uncle and intervened in the mating process of the herds, thereby walking away with a large number of choice animals (Genesis 30:25-43). But in leaving Laban, Jacob ran into his past in the person of his cheated brother Esau and a host of armed men (Genesis 32:6).

Sending his family and flocks ahead, Jacob remained behind alone. Without warning, he was attacked by an unknown assailant. It says they wrestled. Jacob had to fight whether he wanted to or not. At one point Jacob's assailant put Jacob's thigh out of joint (and the text implies it didn't take much effort). Jacob refused to let go, not in an attempt to bully or force a blessing from God, but because he desperately knew he was at the mercy of both his assailant and Esau.

Not only did he cling tenaciously out of pain, but somehow it began to dawn on Jacob that his opponent wasn't merely a man. When Jacob said he wouldn't let go until he received a blessing, he was saying what God had been waiting to hear all along: Jacob could no longer work the angles. Only God could deliver him, in this helpless condition, from Esau. Jacob had already met God in his dream at Bethel. But helplessness brings God's voice and touch deep into the darkness of our lives, where we may have been slow and even resistant to hear it.

I Did This to Myself

Going on, Paul said that we "were dead in our trespasses. . . ." Trespass speaks of deliberately crossing known boundaries; it means knowing wrong but doing it anyway. Breaking God's laws is far more serious than merely breaking the rules of someone who is bigger than we are and who will slap our wrist. God's law is woven into the moral fabric of the universe. Breaking it is like arguing with gravity; we do so at our peril. Actions have consequences. While we may not like the consequences of a course of action, we cannot avoid them.

In the aftermath of our "barn door" moments, we must live with the knowledge that, in some way, "I did this to myself." Western society indulges in massive denial to numb itself against facing this fact. We deny personal responsibility and shunt the blame onto someone or something else: "I'm not responsible. I'm a product of my sociological environment or a dysfunctional family. I'm a victim of societal injustice. *I* am not responsible; someone else is to blame." While all these things can bring negative pressure on anyone's life, they do not negate our personal responsibility for our lives and actions.

We also try to deny guilt. A radio talk show host recently said he believed guilt to be the most useless, even damaging, experience in the human situation. He has a lot of company. Since much of society has abandoned any notion of absolute values, people are free to shape their values in their own image. When right and wrong are no longer rooted in absolutes but in my own self-serving perception, guilt becomes something I can dismiss.

On top of this, the muscles of the self-esteem movement in its secular expression poise flexed against anything except the flattering airbrushed perceptions of esteem we love to whisper in our own ears. We're told not to listen to negative or unpleasant perspectives that keep us from feeling good about ourselves. Not feeling good about ourselves seems to be the only sin the gurus of humanistic self-esteem will acknowledge.

The self-esteem of much of Western society has been crushed to powder. But sparing people guilt is no way to cure the problem, for guilt is to the soul what pain is to the body. While no one loves pain, it signals us that something is wrong. Biblically, guilt is never primarily an emotion. It's an objective legal concept describing willful disobedience of God's unchanging law. Emotions are not a necessary factor. Spiritually, trespassers stand guilty whether they feel guilty or not. But if we are sensitive to God, have any love for Him at all, we cannot trespass against Him without also feeling guilty. Human conscience is an inner moral barometer. It may not always read completely true, but guilt feelings are trying to tell us that something specific is wrong.

It hurts beyond words to realize our own responsibility for the death of a marriage, parental failures, a job firing, or lost opportunities due to poor decisions or pure selfishness. How often we may have yearned to go back and relive some situation differently! But once a "barn door" moment strikes, once a course of action has been taken and consequences follow, we cannot go back. We must take a hard look at ourselves and own up by saying, "I did this to myself."

If we do not, one or two things may follow. We may continue to keep dodging accountability for our lives, thereby guaranteeing possible explosions in our future. Or we may reach the point where the guilty feel no guilt. Paul warns that the guilty can become callous (Ephesians 4:19), that the conscience can be seared as if by a hot iron (1 Timothy 4:2). When the guilty before God have hardened themselves against their guilt, they become a grievous heartache to God and a risk to all around them. We stand always in danger of drifting toward becoming one of them.

I'm Trapped

"Barn door" moments leave us feeling trapped in at least two ways. Paul says we are "dead in our trespasses and sins." To sin means simply to fall short. My best just isn't good enough to pull things out, to turn things around, to divert or escape the consequences of my thoughts and actions. We cannot live so as to please the holy God who will be our judge.

The apostle Paul had to chew on this as part of his coming to Christ. He was the perfect example of a man who had worked both hard and very carefully to put the pieces of his life together (see Philippians 3:4-6). He had been born into a pure Hebrew family line in the tribe of Benjamin. He had studied under Gamaliel, a renowned teacher of the day. He had affiliated with the most conservative party of Judaism, the Pharisees. As one of them, he had devoutly kept the law as best a man could as well as the minutely detailed regulations contained in the Hebrew traditions of the elders. His passion of belief boiled over hotly against all those who differed in belief and attempted to pollute his pure faith in the God of Abraham. While others merely talked, Paul acted. With warrants in hand from the authorities, he hunted down and helped imprison these new heretics who followed the teachings of Jesus of Nazareth. Had his life and history gone on undisturbed, Paul might well have risen through the ranks of the Sanhedrin, the Hebrew supreme court. He strained every atom of his being to please God and do right.

That was what really drove him into a frenzy about the followers of Jesus. He had imprisoned them and been a consenting witness as a mob killed one of them, a man named Stephen. Everything Paul wanted with all his heart in a relationship with God these followers of Jesus had. Everything he had worked, sweated, and strained for yet failed to attain these followers of Jesus enjoyed to overflowing. This fueled his hatred for them even more. Paul had been authorized by the Jews to hunt these people down as far away as Damascus. Of course, on the way, Jesus Christ confronted him. Christ said, "It is hard for you to kick against the goads" (Acts 26:14). Paul couldn't choke down the idea that his best wasn't good enough. His pride had to be broken on the road to Damascus.

The other side of the trapped feeling in our "barn door" moments comes in the discovery that, not only is my best not good enough, but I'm in deeper than I thought. Paul looked within himself and said to the Ephesians and to us, "We too all formerly lived in the lusts of our flesh, indulging the desires of the flesh and of the mind" (Ephesians 2:3). Jeremiah spoke more bluntly and cut even deeper when he wrote, "The heart is more deceitful than all else and is desperately sick; who can understand it?" (Jeremiah 17:9). A superficial theology of sin makes for shallow, vulnerable Christians. Sin is not merely something that we do that God evaluates on some kind of graduated scale. *Sin is something cherished and rooted within the deepest part of us.* Richard Lovelace sagely writes:

In its biblical definition, sin cannot be limited to isolated instances or patterns of wrongdoing; it is something much more akin to the psychological complex: an organic network of compulsive attitudes, beliefs and behaviour deeply rooted in our alienation from God. Sin originated in the darkening of the human mind and heart as man turned from the truth about God to embrace a lie about him and consequently a whole universe of lies about creation.[6]

Sin has compelling power and a life of its own. It is the uncharted blackness within that makes every twisted evil we think ourselves incapable of a reality if the circumstances are right. It is humbling and frightening to reach down in our heart with our own good opinion of ourselves, our inner strength, and our education, and not touch bottom.

Paul also finds our trappedness rooted in the strength of pressures without—

> . . . in which you formerly walked according to the course of this world, according to the prince of the power of the air, of the spirit that is now working in the sons of disobedience (Ephesians 2:2).

Human sin is buttressed and reinforced through Satan's manipulative control over cultures and their institutions. Racial hatred and materialistic expectations that cater to self while ignoring the poor aren't just individual things but sin patterns woven into the fabric of society. We live in a fallen world and we reverberate to its sometimes supernaturally directed pressures as a violin string trembles under the bow of a master.

Amidst the helplessness, blame, and feelings of being trapped, our "barn door" moments finally can leave us with a sense of being deserving of consequences, of failure. Paul's way of expressing it is to say we are "children of wrath" (Ephesians 2:3). This goes beyond my being responsible for consequences; it admits honestly that it is right that the consequences have shaken down as they have. It says, "Not only did I bring this upon myself, but I deserve this."

God's Heart in Our Worst Times

Whatever our opinions of God may be, they pale in comparison to His opinions of us. Michael Green wryly quotes, "It is not what I think of God, but what God thinks of me that matters."[7] This is especially true in our naked moments. Helplessness, blame, and failure tend to lay us on our face before God. What kind of God handles the raw exposed nerves of the implosions of my soul? Paul says One who is "rich in mercy." A sure litmus test of character is the handling of abundance. Some who have riches hoard them. An investment broker told me how difficult it was to get new millionaires to take risks. "They want to hang on to enough to still say they have a million dollars." Others spend but only on themselves.

Like many of us, God spends lavishly on those He loves. The incarnation shows that God refused to play it safe. Christ took on flesh and immersed Himself in man's fallen estate all the way to the cross. One preacher put it this way: "When Christ died on the cross, God's pockets were empty." He spent it all; He could give no more than all of Himself.

The mercy of God is never bestowed at room temperature. Paul says God's mercy is "because of His great love with which He loved us" (Ephesians 2:4). The love of God flows from His heart like lava from a volcano, razing and melting everything in its path. In Scripture, compassion is an urgent, insistent tenderness toward the downtrodden, helpless, or wounded.

It burns in Jesus like the filament of a light bulb. It waxes as hotly in His heart for the masses as for individuals. Jesus could survey a large crowd of people, and where others saw only a sea of blank faces, He saw the misdirected groping of spirits aching for God—so much so that they sometimes overlooked basic needs such as food (see Matthew 9:36; 14:14; Mark 8:2).

But the great love of God flamed up in Jesus for individuals as well. He felt it toward a leper shunned by everyone (Mark 1:40,41). Jesus was going up to Jerusalem for the last time. As the crowd left Jericho and accompanied Jesus, the crowd thronged beside Him, praising and cheering. Two blind men risked being trampled by the masses to cry out to the Master. The crowd tried to hush the men. Stark need always dashes the reverie of selfish feeding masquerading as worship. How tragic and true it is that God's people in the midst of worship can be so empty of what Jesus is so full of!

But Jesus was not so intoxicated with men's praise (as we might be) that He couldn't hear two cries laced with anguish over the din of dull, fickle masses. Jesus had compassion and healed the two men. The heart of God did not have to wait for Calvary to bleed. The cross marked the fatal hemorrhage from bleeding that began with man's fall in the Garden of Eden.

Fruits of His Mercy

Mercy from God runs much deeper than the bestowal of forgiveness; mercy breeds incredible things in any life where the Spirit of God smooths grace like salve on wounds. When seen rightly, mercy is never something we merely receive and then walk away; it lays claim on and blooms within us.

> God, being rich in mercy, because of His
> great love with which He loved us, even when
> we were dead in our transgressions, made us

alive together with Christ (by grace you have
been saved) (Ephesians 2:4,5).

God made us alive in the midst of our death. Life at His
hand is a substantive quality infused through the Holy
Spirit. It is based on our relationship with Jesus Christ, and
it is not only something people can see but also admire. As
a college freshman, I remember my first look at Jesus Christ
living in human personality. I had grown up around church
and had my own beliefs. I had no interest at all in the
dormitory Bible studies going on.

But I went anyway, for a particular reason. Living four
to a room gives a close look at what makes people tick. As I
saw the daily lives of the regulars at the Bible study, I
couldn't escape seeing something utterly different in their
lives. I couldn't explain it, but I began to long for whatever
it was. Their lives radiated Christ's life; He made them
alive.

For all its wild and woolly edges, the Jesus movement
showcased God's life-giving mercy reaching into the counterculture and the college campus. Religion didn't grab
those caught up in it; they weren't looking for religion.
They looked for truth, reality, justice, love, and meaning
but had foraged up all the wrong alleys looking for the right
things. Jesus supernaturally indwelling human personality allured these young people like bees to nectar. The
movement had its shipwrecks, oddities, and eccentricities.
But as from raw marble, God's mercy culled some real
monuments for His kingdom that still stand strong in the
church today.

God's mercy not only brings life but enables change.
Paul hints at this by saying, "God raised us up with Him,
and seated us with Him in the heavenly places" (Ephesians
2:6). The downside of change is often easy to see—the
behaviors I want to stop, the things I want to escape and
leave behind. But change ensconced in God's mercy is not
only change *from* but *to*. God certainly wants to deliver us
from much of what we were before Christ, but He also has

clear ideas of what we are to become. Just a few verses farther along Paul notes, "We are His workmanship, created in Christ Jesus for good works, which God prepared beforehand that we should walk in them" (Ephesians 2:10).

One day a father realized that his preschool children needed a toybox. (Stepping on a squeaky bunny in our bare feet at two in the morning presses the inevitable upon us.) The father went to a friend who was a carpenter, thinking that it would pose no problem for his friend to nail together some plywood into a bin. The carpenter said he would be glad to build a toybox for the family.

Weeks passed and they heard nothing from their friend. Not wanting to seem impatient, they refrained from phoning for awhile but finally couldn't wait. The carpenter's wife said her husband just finished it and they could pick it up that night. What the family found that night standing in the middle of the carpenter's workshop was far from a plywood bin. A hardwood toy chest, hand-carved and elaborately painted, stood in front of them. Feeling awe as well as embarrassment, the father stammered both his thanks and almost an apology—that they hadn't really expected anything so beautifully done. The carpenter's wife reproached him by saying, "But you must understand that Gus is a cabinetmaker. He could never, as you say, 'throw a box together.' His pride would not permit it."[8]

God simply will not leave us as we are. The heart of God that overflows with mercy simply will not stop short of transformation. We are His workmanship; He cannot do or give less than His best. He works, carves, sculpts, sands, chisels, and polishes until He sees Himself in His work. Redemption allows no shortcuts, no skimping on effort. God's mercy not only releases us from the penalty of sin; it makes change from the results of sin sure and real.

A Voice from the Bushes

"Barn door" moments make us want to hide—from people, from the world, from God. Adam and Eve needed no long deliberation to know their nakedness, no rehearsing of options before heading for the bushes. In Genesis, God did not ask where they were because He did not know. But God knew that by holding them to an answer, He was holding them accountable.

Anytime a "barn door" moment drives us into the bushes (into hiding, denial, rationalizing, scapegoating, busyness—bushes come in a wide variety), we must answer for why we are there. God knew they were there, and Adam and Eve had no hope for any kind of life until they spoke up and faced Him. So must we. His love is too tenderly fierce to pretend He doesn't see. As we read in Genesis about God's pronouncements, it's easy to overlook the fact that He clothed their nakedness (Genesis 3:21).

He still clothes nakedness; He clothes it with His righteousness. But we must speak up from the bushes. One morning I walked out of a day-care chapel service determined there would never be another "barn door" moment like that again—and there hasn't. But the good intentions that prevent one self-inflicted embarrassing moment aren't strong enough to fend off the repeated ripple of dark muscle that our sinful nature is capable of. We will have many of those times to face.

In feeling sewn up with helplessness, blame, and failure there is but one avenue to take, and that is to the cross of Christ. There in our mess we can embrace God, knowing He will meet us in mercy and cover us with Himself. But remember that God's mercy and grace are blood-bought gifts extended only to those who stop trying to hide and who own their spiritual nakedness before Him.

7

Mentoring God's Way

I learned jazz from jazzmen. Records were my textbooks; my ears took in every bar and solo. I spent hours running my fingers over the strings of my bass until they bled, listening to the interrelated chord patterns and dissecting them. But there were still things in my head that I couldn't transfer to my fingertips. Seeing jazz live really helped. Watching how pros actually pulled off what I heard from recordings put me in awe of their skill and spurred me on to work harder, especially since they were so personally encouraging.

But nothing beat studying and playing with them. Val lived up to the stereotype of a "beatnik" jazzman. He wore sunglasses all the time and showed up at the house with his dirty laundry slung over his shoulder. He washed it at the Laundromat across the alley while I had my lesson. His whole life pulsated with the rhythm of the music that captured my heart. Sometimes he would bring his accordion and we would play together. My simple bass lines sounded great embellished by the fountain of music that bubbled out of his accordion, out of his heart. "Dave," he would say with eyes glowing over a broad "Cheshire cat" grin, "It's got to swing or it's nowhere!"

Later I studied with Mike, who easily would remember me as the worst student he ever had. Mike understood that real freedom came with discipline; he studied in Europe with jazz bassists of international renown. He drilled me on the mechanics he knew I needed to master.

Finally, "Coach," my first jazz band director, taught me about striving for excellence in enhancing the playing of others. I would hang around the upstairs room at the junior high where he taught, hoping he would have a few minutes to noodle around on the piano while I played bass. He always managed to find time.

We call them mentors today; they seem to be all the rage in professional circles. But they've always been around, if by other names. The best way to learn a skill, glean needed wisdom, or work to assimilate admired character traits has always been to find someone who has them. Then we follow and watch as closely as they will allow and listen to as much as they will tell us.

Godliness from God

We learn godliness from God; only He can meet and satisfy all the hungers and desires His Spirit awakens in us. God mentors by revealing Himself to men as He sovereignly oversees the affairs of nations and individuals. In Scripture we can look over His shoulder and into the deepest recesses of the heart to understand how He may work with us. God can select from a vast repertoire of approaches and methods, tailoring each one perfectly to the needs of the individual. But as redemption is outlined in the shape of a cross, we do well to remember that God is no soft, indulgent mentor. God spared Himself nothing; it's unlikely we will be spared much.

Francis Schaeffer once claimed that these are dangerous times in which to be a soft Christian. The winds of our day blow from strange and hostile directions. Living in the status quo of a mediocre church life confined within the granite walls of inviolable traditions may have passed for Christianity before but will betray many in the years ahead. Not only does soft Christianity wither under the rapidly growing pressures of a post-Christian culture, but it fails to show anything of witness. Soft Christianity not only cannot stand, it cannot penetrate.

God looks to mentor oaks. Undergrowth and weeds He leaves to lesser and infernal hands. He works to build lives from nothing that stand into the wind like jutting granite, lives that cut into our times like a rapier's steel, that radiate enough of Christ's love to melt the thickest heart this age may have hardened. Most of us seem a long way from that.

I love the Olympics. It's so moving to watch athletes stand during the award ceremony as the flag of their country goes up and the national anthem plays. I get goose bumps; sometimes my eyes water. While I try to get inside the head of those champion athletes and imagine what they must feel, I will never know the feeling myself. Part of the reason is that I'm 42 years old. But other reasons run deeper. I simply refuse to relinquish pepperoni pizzas washed down with Diet Pepsi, as these food items are essential to survival in Western society. I also believe that people who enjoy running long distances for fun need counseling. While I admire the fruits of all that work and discipline from afar, I'll never taste it because I'm not willing to invest what it takes. I may be anything from preoccupied and overextended to just apathetic and lazy.

God won't let us daydream about His riches without beginning to climb. While most of us will never stand in an Olympic medal presentation, God means for us to attain the spiritual heights that often seem so unattainable. He will finish what He started; God will cull out the oak in us to the amazement of all (including ourselves) and to His praise (2 Corinthians 4:7; Ephesians 1:6,12,14). He has a remedy for our defiance, rebellion, ambivalence, dullness, and contentment with mediocrity. It shocks us to life—or at least to the realization we're dying. It's called brokenness.

Is This Necessary?

Even as a surgeon uses many instruments but still returns repeatedly to the scalpel, brokenness in God's hand does some of the most delicate surgical work in our spiritual lives. While we may shrink from even the sound of it, spiritual brokenness is not something to avoid but to embrace. It is the prize for those longing to know God so intensely that they will endure the heat of His holiness. It is God allowing absolutely nothing, no matter how desirable or respectable, to interfere with His love for us, His work in and through us.

Mental health circles today know about something called "intervention." Intervention sounds rather sterile and clinical, but in truth it can get pretty messy. It's necessary when people refuse to face personal problems that have become serious. Friends, family, and others forcibly confront the person in denial not only with the truth of the problem but with the pain the problem has caused.

I served on the board of a treatment center handling compulsive gamblers. One man came in for help after losing two houses to the bank. His wife pleaded with him to get help, but he refused to admit his need. The economic ravages suffered by his family couldn't shake his well-oiled rationalizations. Finally one day his wife sat down at the kitchen table. No yelling or screaming. No pleading. In a flat, emotionless voice she said, "We can't take anymore. I've bought a gun. It's loaded and I've hidden it where you'll never find it. If you hurt this family once more with your gambling, I'll wait until you're asleep one night and put a bullet through your head." The man began to get the picture and sought help.

Brokenness is God's intervention. He orchestrates people, events, and circumstances to confront us with truth about ourselves that we've gone to great lengths to avoid. In brokenness, we take an unvarnished look at what we are without God's hand on our life. We see what we have inflicted on ourselves and others. We see how thread-bare, ravaged, and wasted our lives have become at our own hands. We see the sober, horrible realities of judg-ment and hell and know that we're powerless to avoid or face them. Broken people are desperately pliant in God's hand; they now listen eagerly to the One they have in other, more self-indulgent times found convenient to ignore. In brokenness we learn repeatedly that God's love will hound us right to the edge of death—especially those of us who blindly seem so much at home there.

A friend of mine has a saying: When in doubt, use a bigger hammer. As we encounter brokenness, at times it may seem too much to bear. God's hammers, while diverse, can get pretty big. He only employs them, only intervenes, when we leave Him no other choice.

Nuts and Bolts of Brokenness

A college friend once said, "If you can't graph it, what good is it?" While this works great with mathematics, abstractions are tougher to chart and diagram. But spiritual brokenness has recognizable characteristics and parame-ters. Brokenness is always mediated by the Holy Spirit. Jesus promised, "He, when He comes, will convict the world concerning sin, and righteousness, and judgment" (John 16:8). Like white corpuscles patrolling the blood-stream for infection and disease, the Holy Spirit broods watchfully over our spirit, knowing no détente with any-thing that lifts its hand against God.

That God's Spirit serves as the vehicle for the mediation of brokenness is terribly important. The promise of the Spirit is real, but we tend to bend it into the shape of our times. Wanting instant gratification and valuing transcen-dent experience over intellect, many people covet certain aspects of the Holy Spirit's work while forgetting others.

We may want the supernatural aspects of the Spirit because we think them to be a panacea for our problem. We may be merely curious or have a lust for spiritual power. But we are not free to pick and choose what parts of the Spirit's work we want. The Holy Spirit is not a "thing" but the fully integrated third Person of the Trinity. When we receive Him, we receive all that He is. Praying for His fullness in our lives can be an invitation to more than we expect, as A. W. Tozer notes well:

> Are you sure that you want to be possessed by a Spirit who, while he is pure and gentle and wise, will insist upon being Lord of your life? Are you sure you want your personality to be taken over by One who will require obedience to the written Word? Who will not tolerate any of the self-sins in your life: self-love, self-indulgence? Who will not permit you to boast or strut or show off? Who will take the direction of your life away from you and will reserve the sovereign right to test you and discipline you? Unless you can answer an eager "Yes" to these questions, you do not want to be filled. You want the thrill or the victory or the power, but you do not really want to be filled with the Spirit.[9]

Because God speaks through His Spirit into our brokenness, we should note some things in the tone and direction of His voice. The Holy Spirit always attacks sin; He never denigrates the person. Conviction and shame at His hand never attach to a person's being. Even in sin, we are God's creation that He still believes worth redeeming. We live in times that pulverize people; millions have no sense of self-worth or intrinsic value. These panel their souls with boxcar-loads of guilt and blame, often undeserved.

On top of this, Satan works both individually and through facets of Western culture to continually accuse and slander any and all vestiges of a sound estimate of worth and responsibility. When the voices in our heart seem to say, "You're no good. What a worthless loser! How can God forgive you again or use you?"—that is not the voice of the Holy Spirit. He never falls on us in one crushing load like a wall of bricks; He never trashes us. He does slice with the lean precision of the scalpel; His first cut can come without warning or anesthesia and may take our breath away. But it is always with neither mistake nor wasted motion; He cuts only at that which, if left, will kill us.

Explosion of Brokenness

Another dimension of spiritual brokenness is its centrality. Brokenness never occurs on the side of our life; it explodes to the foreground of our life from the core of our being and overshadows everything. The details may vary; the occurrence may be trivial or cataclysmic. But when God confronts us on the ground of our inner deadness and idolatry, everything pales in significance.

We just don't see things the way God does. A little boy was sent to his room for not eating his prunes. The boy's mother told him (mistakenly, I believe) that God wouldn't like it. Later a storm blew up and the little boy stood at his window taking in the lightning and thunder. The crash of the storm rattled the windowpanes. Unafraid, the boy shook his head and thought, "All that fuss over some lousy prunes!"

With some sin, we can't seem to really see what the big deal is. It's not that the Bible is wrong; it's just that some sin seems to be pretty low-grade stuff. Lying and covetousness seem to pale in comparison to rape and murder. Some sin does have greater capacity to inflict pain and suffering, but while some types of sin seem to loom over others, God grades by a different standard.

The deeds of the flesh are evident, which
are: immorality, impurity, sensuality, idolatry,

sorcery, enmities, strife, jealousy, outbursts of anger, disputes, dissensions, factions, envying, drunkenness, carousing, and things like these, of which I forewarn you just as I have forewarned you that those who practice such things shall not inherit the kingdom of God (Galatians 5:19-21).

Do you not know that the unrighteous shall not inherit the kingdom of God? Do not be deceived; neither fornicators, nor idolaters, nor adulterers, nor effeminate, nor homosexuals, nor thieves, nor the covetous, nor drunkards, nor revilers, nor swindlers shall inherit the kingdom of God (1 Corinthians 6:9,10).

God simply doesn't grade sin; it all stands as an offense to Him. All sin kills and destroys that which is precious to Him. When we don't see things from God's perspective, we don't see someone deeply cut in spirit over something comparatively minor. The occasion, degree, and type of sin make no difference.

In 1953, God's Spirit moved deeply in what was then the Congo (Zaire). A little boy, deeply convicted and grieving over the theft of a razor blade, found no rest until he went to the shopkeeper, confessed, and repaid the few cents. A few years earlier in Scotland, a man came to Christ under the powerful influence of a move of God's Spirit in the Hebrides Islands. After his conversion, he had to return to America and work for a year to make restitution for things he had done. In spiritual brokenness, God educates us as to the severity and depth of all sin against the backdrop of His holiness. The occasion may seem trivial, but God uses such things to press us deeply and move us to action, to repentance.

Some things we can sense coming. Scientists tell us earthquakes can be anticipated. Tornadoes too. But while both break without much warning, the final release is the culmination of a process. The onset of brokenness is gradual. As brokenness involves cleansing for service as well as restoration of relationship, it is not surprising that as we look behind the scenes we shall find many people greatly used by God to be broken people. The circumstances and raw materials of their life and times become arranged under God's hand like a carefully stacked bonfire waiting for the match.

Our sense of emptiness without God, our ignored and unknown hardness against Him, our heartache for the lostness of those around us, our anger against the evil of our day—all these and more always lie intertwined in the life of someone God is breaking. In addition is what Scripture calls "the fullness of time"—when God arranges all the externals, carefully staging rulers and nations to powerfully change things for His glory.

Martin Luther and John Wesley didn't set out to create the large movements (the Protestant Reformation and First Great Awakening) associated with them. They both knew deep anguish of spirit that lasted for years. Their desire for truth roared within like a prairie fire. Their deep agitation and longing of spirit dovetailed with the ferment of the times—a church in decay and a new nationalistic spirit among nobles and masses buried beneath poverty and ignorance.

At times God brings societies and cultures to a flash point waiting to be sparked by one life. He penetrates towns, workplaces, and neighborhoods the same way. The process can run in a million different directions but the end is always the same: to bring us to the point where we lose all our deeply ingrained inclination to tell God what to do with our lives, to melt down all resistance to His will.

Shapes of the Craft

Like a master carpenter, God fits the tool to the job.

Some planes require two hands and cut deep. Others, like those used by violin and guitar makers, fit on the end of a finger and make delicate, refined cuts. He always tailors His method to the individual, especially when it comes to needed sanding and scouring. While a wide array of approaches lies under God's hand, we will only embarrass ourselves and frustrate both our growth and our usefulness if we are sensitive only in some special directions.

Of all the mentors of brokenness, our sin stands unsurpassed as a guide to powerful and fruitful living for God. Sin indulged, denied, or ignored teaches nothing; it only enslaves and erodes as surely as hard rain washes away good soil. But sin broken in confession becomes an able teacher. To look hard at sin engaged and grappled with is to flood the contours of the soul with light. We learn about our own weaknesses; we gain new respect for them.

A group I was in interviewed a candidate for a ministry position. We discussed experience, education, and other things. Finally I asked, "What are your weaknesses? You don't have to tell me, but I need to know that you're aware of them because this ministry will stress every one of them to the breaking point." Sin not only blinds us as to the truth and power of the gospel (2 Corinthians 4:4), but it blinds us to its own inroads and patterns in our lives as well. We miss what can be painfully evident to others.

But Satan won't. I've talked with many people whose lives teetered on the edge of destruction due to sin they never dreamed they would encounter. Confession not only identifies my sin but retraces its entrenchment. I glean wisdom into the onset of temptations, their timings, and their varied strengths. I become sensitive to situations where it is futile, stupid, and even dangerous to trust myself. How badly this kind of practical wisdom is needed in churches where even Christians of long standing grope and flounder in the dark, with seemingly no grip on where fighting back might begin!

Bedrock for Change

We piddle at change. Resolve evaporates with the fumes of good intention. I will muddle through the motions of dieting for a couple of weeks. That first flush of energy that got me exercising for a few days fizzles out as daily busyness chokes out the time like encroaching weeds. Genuine time with God loses the battle with sleep, or else I drag into it dopey and dull or rush through it so I emerge on the other side emptier than if I had not spent the time at all. Even more difficult to bring about is deep change over emotional response patterns ingrained over years, attitudes reinforced by culture, experience, and pain, habits worn deep into my performance by countless repetitions.

Brokenness brings massive reorientation crashing into our lives. We undergo a reality shift; life never again seems the same. Things we once thought important we drop like old rags; change we failed at or refused to see as necessary we embrace like an old friend. Heart attacks get people on diets, make them give up smoking, and motivate them to take up exercise. Breakdowns speedily press on us and our calendars the importance of primary relationships—sometimes excruciatingly restored through painful apologies—and the necessity of time away from the over-scheduling.

Saul of Tarsus was a brilliant, driven man. Possessed by a skewed zeal, he rose rapidly in all the things the world covets: position, prestige, and power. Saul lived near the combustion point, as driven people do, and at high throttle —too hot in pursuit to ask if the goal is worthy or to wonder exactly what is burning so deep inside to make us push ourselves so hard.

Then one day Saul of Tarsus met Jesus Christ. Meeting Jesus Christ always holds surprises and even danger for those who spend a lot of energy fighting against Him. Anyone can strut as bold as brass against Jesus Christ as long as Jesus doesn't show up. When Jesus said to him, "Saul, Saul, why are you persecuting Me?" (Acts 9:4), He so much as said, "Saul, you have pressed My people terribly. It's time you tested your mettle on Me." As the light vanished and the voice faded, Saul's traveling companions led the blind pile of pieces that had once been Saul of Tarsus down the road by the hand to Damascus. There he sat, blind and helpless, without food or water, for three days (and he didn't know it would be just three days!).

Two things happened to Saul. First, his carefully constructed world and view of life were crushed like an eggshell so the bitter insides could run out. Regaining his sight at the hands of Ananias, Saul was a changed man. Christ's persecutor now preached Christ. Even for all the miracles it had seen, the early church needed persuasion to accept their new brother. The change was so radically swift and they had so much to forgive.

Paul later looked back and saw things differently.

> . . . even though I was formerly a blasphemer and a persecutor and a violent aggressor. And yet I was shown mercy, because I acted ignorantly in unbelief (1 Timothy 1:13).

> It is a trustworthy statement, deserving full acceptance, that Christ Jesus came into the world to save sinners, among whom I am foremost of all (1 Timothy 1:15).

What he thought was an attempt to please God was in reality blasphemy. In confessing sin, the Holy Spirit shows us what our sin does to God. We may regret the consequences of our sin, or we may only regret getting caught, but until we see that our sin wounds God, we haven't completely seen it. Not only did Paul see what his sin had really done to God, but he saw that he still had a twisted taste for it.

> I know that nothing good dwells in me, that is, in my flesh; for the wishing is present

in me, but the doing of the good is not. For the
good that I wish, I do not do; but I practice the
very evil that I do not wish (Romans 7:18,19).

Jesus Christ pounded the Pharisee out of Paul, and
sometimes we need that as well. Jesus wasn't killed by
people like Annas, Caiaphas, and Pilate. Scripture draws
back the veil revealing the real culprits.

He was pierced through for our transgres-
sions, He was crushed for our iniquities; the
chastening for our well-being fell upon Him,
and by His scourging we are healed. All of us
like sheep have gone astray, each of us has
turned to his own way; but the Lord has caused
the iniquity of us all to fall on Him (Isaiah
53:5,6).

From a country church in Kentucky to the steel and
glass of a suburban megachurch, we can walk into a worship service anywhere knowing that the people who killed
Jesus are there; there simply isn't one respectable person in
the place.

The Holy Spirit brokers deep change at steep rates. He
often must break up the pavement of superficial respectability, especially the religious kind. Genuine lasting
change comes in the life where spiritual brokenness bites
deep.

8

‿‿‿

Must I Get
My Way?

One of my favorite book titles of all time has got to be *How to Be Your Own Selfish Pig*. We live in times when many people already seem to know how to be selfish. The cult of self-interest gathers converts daily around the altars of the religion of "need." I simply take my most pressing desires and redefine them as "needs." How could even God deny me my legitimate "needs"?

Much church-growth literature currently advises not to press people for commitment, as certain age groups don't make commitments easily. The truth is that the only commitments we Americans have trouble making are those that threaten the passionate commitments we instinctively make to our own desires. One biblical measure of evil times is that men will be lovers of themselves (2 Timothy 3:2). When various spokespersons for the New Age movement claim that we are gods, they only make embarrassingly plain what we subliminally already embrace: Left alone, we fill with ourselves.

God's mentoring of His life through brokenness will place us in situations where we simply don't get what we want. He will incarnate in some way John the Baptist's perceptive realization that "He must increase, but I must decrease" (John 3:30). Through small daily frustrations and larger disappointments, God will be pointing out to us both that getting our way is too important and that delighting in His way is not nearly important enough. He does this not to torment or badger us but to shake us free of the delusion that happiness means getting what we want and that's all.

I was a guest on a radio talk show. A listener phoned in to say that she had wanted a better job and had prayed for it. She got one, and said that the Bible promised that God will give us the desires of our heart. American culture, success-oriented and materialistic, sees blessings as good things (interpreted as things I want) happening or coming to me. But what Psalm 37:4 actually says is this: "Delight yourself in the Lord, and He will give you the desires of your heart." Our natural bent is to use God to obtain our desires. Delighting in God purifies our desires to where God can grant them freely, knowing that our delight is in Him and not in what He can do for us. Then our desires are no longer idolatrous.

Sometimes brokenness means exposing our spiritual pride. The truth is that few of us are as spiritually mature as we think. We tend to overstate ourselves at times; we get in over our heads or are out of our league without knowing it.

Peter, for example, basked in the moment. Jesus had just been asking questions examining the disciples' depth of perception as to who He was. Suddenly Peter's mind, enlightened by God, snapped together all those intuitive pieces of who Jesus was into a sharp, clear picture. Straightforward and clean, Peter answered, "Thou art the Christ, the Son of the living God" (Matthew 16:16; see also Mark 8:29). In front of all the others, Jesus showered him with warm commendation as well as delivering strong prophetic words. The instant God reveals something remarkable to us or uses us in a special way is a dangerous moment. If we're not appropriately humbled, we swell like toads. Once we have heard from God (or think we have), we can sometimes have trouble listening to other people.

In the afterglow of this moment, Jesus taught His disciples very pointedly about His death and resurrection. While none of them wanted to hear about the death of the One they loved, Peter expressed his feelings in words. Actually, he did more; Peter *rebuked* Jesus by saying, "God forbid it, Lord! This shall never happen to You" (Matthew 16:22; see also Mark 8:32,33). Jesus let Peter know in an instant that Peter had crossed a dangerous line. A day or so earlier God may have spoken to Peter, but now Satan was speaking through him. Jesus, in effect, said, "You're mouthing the lie of the devil. You've forgotten who we both are. Stop it!" The one who had been shown great things from God was now an obstacle that Jesus had to knock out of the way to continue to the cross.

How Are We Hearing?

Nobody hears God clearly all the time. Nobody obeys God perfectly. When we begin to strut in our spirit, to distance ourselves from other Christians because they don't know God as well as we do, or when we assume that because we've been Christians longer than someone else we must have the answers, God engineers a vital part of our education that always stings a little.

Among the seven deadly sins of medieval lore was sloth—a state of hard-bitten, joyless apathy of spirit. There is a lot of it around today in Christian circles; the symptoms are personal spiritual inertia combined with critical cynicism about churches and supercilious resentment of other Christian initiative and enterprise. Behind this morbid and deadening

Embracing God

condition often lies the wounded pride of one who thought he knew all about the ways of God in providence and then was made to learn by bitter and bewildering experience that he didn't.[10]

I've heard hundreds, probably thousands, of testimonies. People have asked for prayer and have praised God for any number and variety of victories. Individuals said God was leading them into a major change of direction—a new career, a marriage, a call to ministry, etc. God's leading and anointing were there, they claimed, and so these people set off with flags flying.

But the career, the marriage, the ministry broke to pieces in six months. What happened? As we live our lives in a hostile spiritual environment, attack that undermines authentic direction from God can strike from any direction. But could the collapse stem from our being wrong about God's leading in the first place? Regardless of good intentions, doing something for Jesus Christ that He doesn't want done is still disobedience.

I've never seen someone stand up and say, "I know you heard me claim that God was leading us to move to Michigan to start that new ministry. It fell apart because we were wrong. We ran on emotions. We avoided people who would have held us accountable for our motives. We refused to see the obvious. We're sorry for any reproach our foolishness has brought on Christ and you, His church. Pray that we'll be more humble and teachable."

God won't allow us to hide our shabbiness behind titles, positions, and degrees (earned, honorary, or bought). Jesus warned about becoming enamored with titles; they can fool us into believing we're something we're not.

We never outgrow the shadow of the cross. Earthly clout and privilege mean nothing. A publicist for a Christian publisher related how one author must have first-class accommodations, a limousine, and all kinds of first-class amenities, and throws tantrums if these aren't provided.

God simply won't let that go on unchecked in us. The more visible or more crucial our ministry to His kingdom, the fiercer His pruning of our pride. The first step toward being filled with Christ is realizing how full of ourselves we are.

Getting Love or Giving It?

Love is a problem; both the world around us and Scripture think so. But they approach it from opposite directions. For talk shows, soap operas, and millions of lonely people who run classified ads, the problem is to find love—to find someone to love me. In Scripture, the problem of love is learning to give it to others. We don't come by this naturally.

> ... our relationships with others easily become needy and greedy, sticky and clinging, dependent and sentimental, exploitative and parasitic, because without the solitude of heart we cannot experience the others as different from ourselves but only as people who can be used for the fulfillment of our own, often hidden, needs.[11]

As Christians we are commanded to love everyone without excuse or exception. If we've never wanted to just throw our hands in the air and quit at this, maybe we've never felt the sheer weight of it.

> I say to you who hear, love your enemies, do good to those who hate you, bless those who curse you, pray for those who mistreat you (Luke 6:27,28).

> Love your enemies, and do good, and lend, expecting nothing in return; and your reward will be great, and you will be sons of the Most

High; for He Himself is kind to ungrateful and evil men (Luke 6:35).

If someone says, "I love God," and hates his brother, he is a liar; for the one who does not love his brother, whom he has seen, cannot love God, whom he has not seen. And this commandment we have from Him, that the one who loves God should love his brother also (1 John 4:20,21).

We just don't have this love in us naturally. Our love, left to itself, runs along human lines. While it runs deep along family lines and among friends, it still runs dry at sometimes crucial moments. Jesus described it well in Luke 6:32: "If you love those who love you, what credit is that to you? For even sinners love those who love them." When someone bites down on me, it's hard not to bite back. What I excel at is cherishing every slight, insult, and abrasive remark, real or imagined, as if they were rubies and emeralds. I lay them on the hearth of my heart, where they glow like red-hot coals. I fan them with every remembrance and rehearsal.

Just a Pantomime

Much of what we have known as Christian love is really a pantomime of the real thing. In church we accept the status quo as the norm; the way it is becomes the way it should be. But that will never be genuinely true until we're in heaven. A religious civility that won't move us across the sanctuary to people we've avoided for months or years infests our churches like an epidemic and stands light-years removed from what Jesus requires of His followers.

The Holy Spirit alone produces God's love in and through us. We can't manufacture it out of our glands, efforts, or good intentions. Its presence marks the rich working of the Spirit and its absence marks a sure quenching of his presence, Person, and influence. Time and again, as we follow

Jesus, we will brokenly discover how little of His love is in us. Jesus Himself will teach us and put us through the rigors of practice.

As a college student I worked in a diagnostic clinic for reading deficiencies run by the school. The last thing school districts in our Appalachian area had were reading specialists. So they sent students with suspected difficulties to us for testing and treatment. We were novices, naive and idealistic. We had no idea of how little we knew. Sometimes we had no idea what we were doing. Groping in the dark, we stared blankly at test scores and diagnostic profiles as if they were hieroglyphics. We were often in over our heads, and yet we desperately wanted to see improvement in these students whom we had grown to love. And many of them did. I remember tearful goodbyes with grateful parents; it would be hard to say who gained more—the students or the clinicians.

Church is such a clinic. Into the church God leads people crushed with sin and pain and desperately in need of love. These often aren't the pretty people we would choose to fill our churches. They can't step right in as Sunday school teachers and may not be substantial givers. Love may be so much a stranger to them that they feverishly clutch any shred of it that crosses their path. They come in all sizes and shapes—some mean, some suicidally depressed.

Jesus populates His church with people who don't have a clue as to how to love these strangers. We Christians find out how quickly our own reservoirs of love for others dry up. Only Jesus in us can love the ones He brings into our lives and churches. And He will give us lots of practice, since the only way to love in Jesus' name is by the hands-on giving away of lots of it.

Tom is a schizophrenic who has been thrown out of or shunned by many other churches. From years of treatment, Tom is a walking encyclopedia of psychotherapy and psychiatric medication. He and I visit regularly, and some of the men in one of our Sunday school classes sit with him in one-on-one Bible study. Once in awhile Tom sits through an entire class or a Wednesday night service. When he can, it's a major accomplishment.

All of us who know Tom agree that he's taught us a lot. We've learned much about people with severe mental illness and the terrible effect that prolonged psychological pain can have. We've learned new respect for psychiatric medication in its ability to sometimes correct chemical imbalance in the brain. We've got better handles on compassion and toughness. Humanly speaking, we're often tough when compassion is required instead; care inconveniences us, and the opportunities for compassion that present themselves often push us toward the second mile when we're not even inclined to walk the first one. Conversely, claims to compassion are sometimes nothing more than a mask to hide our failure of nerve. Compassion is neither coddling nor indulgence. When we withhold correction or accountability for fear of offending, we're not helping.

But most of all, Tom has taught us how empty we are. Christians may never be more like Jesus Christ than when we love someone who repeatedly struggles. We just don't have within us very much of the love he so desperately needs from us. It takes Jesus to love Tom. All of us lean harder on Christ, stretching deeper into His grace, every time he comes.

Drawn to the Cross

The cross of Jesus Christ divides history and the hearts of mankind. The one great polarization of humanity is not political, racial, or ethnic; it is between those drawn to the cross of Jesus Christ and those repelled by it. Christ's cross will always be an active part of every Christian's life.

> He was saying to them all, "If anyone wishes to come after Me, let him deny himself,

and take up his cross daily, and follow Me"
(Luke 9:23).

Paul knew this well.

> I protest, brethren, by the boasting in you,
> which I have in Christ Jesus our Lord, I die
> daily (1 Corinthians 15:31).

Spiritual brokenness means bearing Christ's cross
daily. The cross-bearing that Jesus and Paul refer to means
more than our arthritis and our crotchety in-laws. One side
of it embraces suffering for Christ's sake without complaint. When we willingly endure suffering, hardship, or
deprivation for the sake of the kingdom of God, we carry
Christ's cross.

Jesus could have avoided the cross. At a number of
junctions He could have exercised His power to avoid persecution, arrest, and crucifixion, but He chose not to for the
sake of others. Anyone who follows Jesus Christ should
expect to face the same choice. Frederick Buechner describes it well.

> It is in contrast to all this that what St. Paul
> calls "the foolishness of God" looks so foolish.
> Inspection stickers used to have printed on the
> back "Drive carefully—the life you save may
> be your own." That is the wisdom of men in a
> nutshell.
>
> What God says, on the other hand, is "The
> life you save is the life you lose." In other
> words, the life you clutch, hoard, guard, and
> play safe with is in the end a life worth little to
> anybody, including yourself, and only a life
> given away for love's sake is a life worth living.
> To bring his point home, God shows us a man
> who gave his life away to the extent of dying a
> national disgrace without a penny in the bank

or a friend to his name. In terms of men's wisdom, he was a Perfect Fool, and anybody who thinks he can follow him without making something like the same kind of a fool of himself is laboring under not a cross but a delusion. [12]

Uprooting Self

Cross-bearing also describes the uprooting of our self-centeredness. Paul wrote, "I have been crucified with Christ; and it is no longer I who live, but Christ lives in me; and the life which I now live in the flesh I live by faith in the Son of God, who loved me and delivered Himself up for me" (Galatians 2:20). Not only here but in other references, crucifixion was a slow, painful way to die. It wasn't the only form of capital punishment but one reserved for hardened criminals and for strong points which the authorities wanted to press on the minds of the citizenry. As all the Gospels show, the Romans were professionals who knew their grisly trade well. No one survived a crucifixion; that is Paul's point. The process may have been slow but the end was inescapable.

Regarding our stubborn selfishness, the dying may come hard and slow but the blow has been struck, the nerve cut. Without eradicating personality or nature, God will mine the image of His Son from our clay. We will find the brokenness of the cross pressed into every dimension of our Christian life and experience. If we run from it, we will live the comfortable life of the dead—safe, but empty of all we've looked at in earlier chapters and more.

As the sun sets on the post-Christian West, God will not allow such contentment with contentment stand in the eyes of the world to be mistaken for being Christian. He loves us too much to leave us as we are, the world too much to leave it alone.

9

An Audience of One

The Pope was touring the American heartland. All over the state of Iowa, churches waited excitedly and worked feverishly to spruce up. Many of these beautiful church buildings had been built with the idea in mind that, if the Pope ever came, he would have these churches to speak in. Which church might he visit? Which ones might he actually preach in? The Pope arrived amidst pomp and ceremony, but, wishing to show solidarity with and affinity for the people, he preached on a makeshift platform in a cornfield. Later the diocese bought the cornfield and built a church building on the spot to commemorate his visit.

We sometimes miss God coming and going. We build grand cathedrals for Him to come down and dwell in. Or we erect shrines on places He has already been, as if they could retain His glorious but fleeting presence. The cathedral and the shrine may draw throngs of camera-toting tourists who capture on film the Gothic architecture and the death site of a saint, but neither can contain God; He would much rather indwell the hearts of people than the structures they think they build for Him.

God meets us in strange places and at unusual times. Most encounters with God recorded in the Bible came unexpectedly. People met God when they weren't looking for Him, and in places they least expected. Moses was tending sheep (Exodus 3) and Jacob was trembling at the approach of Esau (Genesis 32). Samuel was awakened out of the sleep of a child (1 Samuel 3). The whirlwind of God found Job awash in suffering (Job 38–41). Jeremiah thought himself to be too young and immature (Jeremiah 1:1-8). God found Daniel in the opulent palace of the king of Babylon (Daniel 1). Jesus shows the same unpredictable variety of encounters.

Aleksandr Solzhenitsyn met God lying in the rotting straw of a Soviet labor camp. Corrie and Betsy ten Boom worshiped in the flea-and-lice-infested barracks of Buchenwald. Augustine's pleasure-seeking life collided with God in a garden where children played nearby. William Booth stumbled over God among the urchins and street rabble of the poorest sections of London. God's Spirit literally ambushed Dwight L. Moody on a busy street.

While God meets people in many places and many ways, we can miss Him right under our nose. We must sidestep at least three major pitfalls as we long to embrace God.

Worship Counterfeits

Worship is tricky business. We can deceive ourselves into thinking we're worshiping by merely being where we think God is. Deeply held attitudes either ingrain the strengths or reinforce the deficiencies of our worship as Christians. Sometimes we cheat ourselves without knowing it. But God does. An old Methodist pastor said once that everyone should take out their brains and stomp on them once in awhile to knock the rust off. Sometimes God helps with just enough of a tap, a little breaking, to knock the rust off our thinking about worship.

First, God warns us of counterfeits to genuine worship. The most dangerous of these is succumbing to appearances without reality. This comes when we're surrounded by all the symbols and accoutrements of the presence of God but the reality isn't there. A magnificent cathedral adorns the heart of the downtown in our metropolitan area. When builders and craftsmen erected these marvelous places, they were making loud statements about God's power and beauty in creation. Even the handiwork of craftsmen working with gold, mahogany, and stained glass testified that the workmen themselves were the handiwork of God. Only He could create a man who could create like this.

At one time people understood and worshiped there. Some still do. But throughout Europe and many cities in the United States, these cathedrals are almost empty on Sundays. Some are closed; I see them boarded up along the expressways.

Even those that are full may not have life. I once worked in a cemetery that had a mausoleum whose trappings would rival many churches. We averaged five additions a week, but those who came were no more alive than those already there. Many churches have the surroundings, the vestments, the ritual, and all the appearances of worship, but the Presence is not there.

In the years following Solomon's dedication of the great temple in Jerusalem, the nation fell into decline and idolatry. Sacrifices fell off. Priests had to be sent home because there weren't enough people coming to worship to support them. The Word of God became neglected at times until the people never missed it. The beautiful furnishings (the bronze laver, the candlesticks, the veil, and the ark of the covenant) never moved.

Could cobwebs have hung like lace from the wing tips of the cherubim over the ark of the covenant? Could a film of dust have covered the mercy seat? Could a heavy religious emptiness be all that remained in a place where the fire of God's glory once drove the priests from the temple?

One sign of this appearance without reality is compliance without understanding. This happens when, in worship, we stand, sit, kneel, sing, pray, read, recite, chant, or do whatever we do merely out of habit. It's an exercise in programmed monotony held within the confines of the printed order of service or liturgy.

A second sign grows out of the first, and that is the lifeless assembly. Fellowship is more than coffee and doughnuts. The shallow conversations on sports, cars, potato salad recipes, and other things that frame our worship services like bookends betray us. One cannot be in the presence of God one minute only to turn glibly to catty remarks about Mildred's hair the next. Conversations on spiritual things actually embarrass or even threaten us. We look askance at those who insist on pressing them.

When we can throw our Christian vocabulary around without experiencing the realities the words describe, we are in serious trouble. When the furniture is in the right place and the language sounds right but we are only becoming more sterile and wooden with every passing week, we're being defrauded by the appearance of religion without the presence of the living God.

The Entertainment Center

A second counterfeit that robs us of real worship is the entertainment center. With our American cultural appetite for spectacle and celebrity, Ringling Brothers has nothing on some of the extravaganzas staged in our churches. This is not to say that worship on a grand scale is unbiblical. The dedication of Solomon's temple (1 Kings 8) and the walls of Jerusalem rebuilt under Nehemiah (Nehemiah 12:27-43) describe worship involving thousands of people. The Bible pictures worship in heaven as something of incredible magnitude.

But where appearance without reality deceives us by allowing us to believe that God is satisfied by habitual religious performance, the entertainment center convinces us that something powerful for God is happening when we may only be witnessing theater or carnival. Even though the music may stir our emotions and we may be dazzled by the talent, God may not be part of things. Talent, production, and celebrity status may eclipse truth and spirit. A prelude to worship is not the same as the pit orchestra bursting into the overture of a Broadway show or the national anthem preceding the first pitch.

The litmus test that reveals the entertainment center for what it is becomes the same as for appearance without reality. What happens when everything is over? When throngs leave our happenings buzzing over talent and technique instead of being deepened in adoration of God, then something is wrong. This also explains why the early church didn't need to spur attendance with contests that culminated with Paul taking a pie in the face or Peter kissing a pig if the goal was reached. God was in their midst; no spectacle, program, or event they could stage could eclipse or surpass Him.

Misguided Focus

Advertising claims to bombard us with hundreds of messages per day. A lot of us work long hours under pressure, leaving few hours for family or outside interests. We sincerely want Christ as the supreme focus of our lives, but it's often difficult to keep our focus sharp amidst the daily things clamoring for our attention.

A second major pitfall to biblical worship is our misguided focus. All my years on the pew side of the pulpit stand framed in need of one kind or another. As a Christian young adult, I drank in everything spiritual I could get. I sat on the edge of my seat like an eager puppy with his spiritual tongue hanging out.

A few years later, after some ministry failure, disillusionment, and burnout, I worked 80 hours a week in two full-time jobs doing nothing more than trying to survive. I came to church tired, often sullen and angry at God, looking for a shred of hope and a scrap of grace. Then it was my intestines that spiritually hung out. And the people who gather to worship in any church are just the same. There's an ache in every heart, a wheelbarrow-load of need in every pew more complex than a ball of snakes.

While our needs are legitimate, they tend to swallow us—especially needs freighted with pain. The more pain, the more we ball up into ourselves, until it can become almost impossible to escape the gravitational pull of our need. But worship is never just coming to get our needs met, to get something to make it through the week. We must lift our gaze higher than our navel until it takes in the Person of God.

Who is the audience in worship? In most traditional settings, we act as if *we* are. Pastors, musicians, dramatists, and others enact worship on the platform up front. We sit back in receiving mode, locked in on getting something out of the service. We never think to ask ourselves one question: Is God getting what *He* came for out of the service? Worship is, among other things, the people of God gathered to give *Him* all the praise and adoration we can render. In worship, God alone is the audience; all of us should be focused on Him. When God receives what He so richly deserves from our worship, we will find all the needs we brought with us touched more deeply in His perfect time than we could have imagined.

Joe Louis Arena in Detroit serves as home for the Detroit Red Wings, who bang the boards and heat up the ice for the rest of the National Hockey League. The Detroit Tigers play baseball at Tiger Stadium, a few minutes away. A few blocks north sits the Fox Theater, a stunning restored venue where top entertainers and shows routinely pack the house. At all three I just walk in, find my seat, and sit down until things start.

We show our misguided focus in worship by failing to recognize the need to prepare. With our own needs uppermost in our mind and the burden for worship transferred to those on the platform, all we have to do is find our seat, sit down, and wait for things to begin. Granted, some people do well just to get there. But is coming into the presence of God the same as entering a stadium or theater?

The temple in Jerusalem had a sacred innermost chamber called the holy of holies. In the holy of holies sat the ark of the covenant, the visible reminder of God's presence among His people. This inner chamber was partitioned off from the rest of the interior by a veil—a double-hung curtain running from floor to ceiling. The curtain hung in two pieces so that no one could catch a random glimpse into the holy of holies.

Even the priest entered the inner chamber only once a year on the Day of Atonement. On that day he came carrying the blood of the Passover lamb to atone for the sins of the nation—blood which would be sprinkled on the mercy seat. Knowing that he was coming into the presence of God, did he prepare for it, or did he just saunter in as if this annual rite were just a routine part of the job?

Preparing for Worship

How do we prepare to worship God? At least three concerns should cross our minds as we pass through the veil. First is the concern of context. Worship never occurs in a vacuum but always fits in the overall context of our relationship with God. Christianity is nothing more than an intimate relationship with God through Jesus Christ. If we are relationally poor with God through the week, worship on Sunday may well disappoint both us and God. If we extend this between-Sundays barrenness into a lifestyle, when we come to worship we will find ourselves looking into the face of One who has become a stranger. A direct correlation exists between the richness of our daily relationship with God and our depth in worshiping Him.

A second concern that prepares us to enter the presence of God is the realization of what makes worship possible in the first place. The priest absolutely could not enter the holy of holies without the blood of atonement. Neither can we.

> Since therefore, brethren, we have confidence to enter the holy place by the blood of Jesus, by a new and living way which He inaugurated for us through the veil, that is, His flesh, and since we have a great priest over the house of God, let us draw near with a sincere heart in full assurance of faith, having our hearts sprinkled clean from an evil conscience and our bodies washed with pure water (Hebrews 10:19-22).

Jesus Christ shed His blood so that I could come freely, even boldly, into God's presence. It is such an amazing privilege for me; it cost Him so much.

A third concern leads us to conscious dependence on the Holy Spirit. He is the facilitator of worship. The apostle John certainly cultivated a deep relationship with God and lived in the privilege of Christ's atonement. In addition, in Revelation 1:10 John says, "I was in the Spirit on the Lord's Day." We need to consciously depend on the Holy Spirit for two reasons: He is the One who takes our attention off ourselves and redirects it toward God, and He enables us to understand what God may be saying.

As a new Christian, I was befriended by a retired missionary who spent 40 years in India. One day she said she received a letter she wanted me to read. As I took it and tried to read it, I couldn't make out a thing. I had never seen worse handwriting and thought maybe I was holding it sideways. But I sure didn't want to look dumb by twisting and turning the letter. Then I saw the woman grin as I had royally fallen for her joke: The letter was written in one of the dialects of India! Left to ourselves, we don't understand the language of heaven.

> Even so the thoughts of God no one knows except the Spirit of God. Now we have received, not the spirit of the world, but the Spirit who is from God, that we might know the things

freely given to us by God, which things we also
speak, not in words taught by human wisdom,
but in those taught by the Spirit, combining
spiritual thoughts with spiritual words. But
a natural man does not accept the things of
the Spirit of God; for they are foolishness to
him, and he cannot understand them, because
they are spiritually appraised (1 Corinthians
2:11-14).

Whether alone or just before worship, a prayer like this
would do all of us good: "Lord, my feelings seem flat. Some
of my need seems big enough to block You from my heart's
view. But as I see the cross and blood of Christ, I'm so
grateful to come to You; it's such a privilege to enter Your
presence. Please lift my gaze through Your Spirit so I may
behold only You. And may He also give me ears to hear so I
miss none of whatever You have to say." Frame it any way
we like, but we're less likely to experience dryness where
there should be life when we prepare to pass through the
veil into God's presence.

The Trap of Our Past

The final pitfall we must escape is the trap of our own
religious past. All of us have a streak of Pharisee in us. We
easily see God moving and working inside parameters we
recognize. But let God step over our well-drawn lines and
we not only have trouble discerning Him but may angrily
insist He isn't there. The Pharisees would have seen themselves as true defenders of the faith. They believed both in
God and the full inspiration of the Scriptures of the day—
the Old Testament. They also believed in angels and the
resurrection of the dead. They attended synagogue regularly, carefully observed the major Jewish feast days, gave
financially, and went to rather stringent lengths to live out
their faith.

But they never imagined that external performance, no
matter how impressive, without genuine love for God from

the heart could never please Him. They became proud and judgmental; these always come hand in hand. If I'm the only one who's pleasing to God, I certainly should be able to spot quickly those who aren't.

The Pharisees never doubted that God was anything less than pleased with them; if He would reveal Himself to anyone, it would surely be to them. And when God spoke, He would speak in ways the Pharisees had always understood, always approved of, and (most important) could always control. All this is exactly why the Pharisees missed Jesus—and why many Christians miss Him in worship today.

Jesus simply won't be squeezed into our ideas of what He ought to be and do. I've known Him for 22 years, and Jesus is infinitely bigger than my meager experience of Him. And while He never violates His Word, everything else is up for grabs. Jesus bursts our bubble repeatedly by leaping into dimensions of Christian living and worship far outside what we can tolerate now—and He calls us to follow Him.

When we refuse out of fear or because we insist that Christ perform in our little boxes, our vision and hunger for Him shrivels quickly and dies! Then something frightening happens: People who believe they love God become His enemies (see John 16:2). These Pharisees who believed the Old Testament and postured as being so religious conspired to murder Jesus as He became a threat to all they held dear.

Smug in Hindsight

History gives us opportunity to be smug. We can look back seeing everything in perspective and knowing all the facts, and reassure ourselves that we would never act like that or be that blind to what God was doing. But the truth is that most major advances of Christianity met their fiercest opposition from within the established church.

The Protestant Reformation found Martin Luther not wanting to begin a new movement but desiring to reform a church that thrust him out. The church locked out those young upstarts John Wesley and George Whitefield, who then preached to the poor, inaugurating the First Great Awakening. Their American colleague, Jonathan Edwards, was thrown out of his church for holding biblical views on the Lord's Supper. William Carey, the father of modern Christian missions, got no cooperation from ministers of his day; they squashed him. Charles Finney, D. L. Moody, William Booth, Charles Spurgeon, Billy Graham, and anybody else God might lead to serve outside whatever box we've come to cherish has known the blistering of the church.

Most churches have an unwritten code that most of the members know. Sometimes every member has his own code. That code describes what kind of music and preaching is Christian, what can and can't happen in worship service, what kind of dress is appropriate, and what constitutes genuine blessing from God. Left to ourselves, we will nail ourselves up in a box of the limits of our experience.

God is bigger than the sum of our accrued experience and belief. He longs to break us out. But to do that, we may have to humbly apologize and take back words we said against other brothers whom we criticized, judged, and slandered merely because we were too blind to recognize God among them. In doing this we may get sniped at by people in our old box, but once our fog of worship confusion lifts, nothing surpasses basking in His presence.

10

~~~

Kneeling in the Fire

Real worship breaks as it lifts. It drains us of pretense and pride, catches us up in the Person of God. It rivets our hopes to His power and majesty and raises deep swells of adoration from our heart that we never knew were there. To worship is to change because we see the living God; no one can behold Him and remain the same. We say we are in His presence all the time. True, but what does it mean to enter the presence of God in worship?

A retired pastor told me of his closest time in God's presence. Then he added, "But I couldn't stand it for long." In college, a few of us gathered in our basement room to end the school year in prayer and with the Lord's Supper. Details aside, somewhere in the middle of our praying together we stepped through a veil into timelessness and into the presence of Jesus Christ. We could no more stand before Him than wax could stand in flame.

Characters in Scripture knew the same experience. Isaiah saw God in the temple the same year King Uzziah died (740 B.C.). The nation was shocked by the swift and horrible death of one on whom God's blessing seemed to rest. Looking for an answer as to why, the nation didn't know it, but the time was ripe for God to speak. In an incredible experience, God made it clear to Isaiah that no one's power, success, or prior obedience gave him license to violate His holy presence or His law (Isaiah 6:1-4). Isaiah was overwhelmed; he learned that the presence of God is nothing to be yawned at.

> Then I said, "Woe is me, for I am ruined! Because I am a man of unclean lips, and I live among a people of unclean lips; for my eyes have seen the King, the Lord of hosts" (Isaiah 6:5).

The apostle John spent some years near the end of his life on the Greek island of Patmos, which served as a Roman penal colony. As is often the case with those imprisoned for their testimony of Jesus Christ, John's heart was as free in prison as in Ephesus, where he had previously ministered. On one particular Sunday, John, apparently engrossed in private worship, was "in the Spirit on the Lord's day" (Revelation 1:10). Suddenly a voice spoke to John from behind, and he turned to see Jesus Christ enthroned in heaven (Revelation 1:12-16).

Were we to see something like these two men saw, how would we react? John may have enjoyed a more intimate relationship with Jesus than the other disciples. He is described uniquely as the disciple Jesus loved (see John 19:26; 20:2; 21:7,20). On their last evening together, John lay with his head on Jesus' chest—just six to eight inches from the face of God!

On seeing Jesus on Patmos, John could have reached back to their privileged relationship: "Jesus! How wonderful to see You. Remember all the great times we had?" But what was John's reaction? "When I saw Him, I fell at His feet as a dead man" (Revelation 1:17).

Other occasions in Scripture reinforce these two. The fiery glory of God filled Solomon's temple at its dedication so that the priests backed out of the temple, unable to stand in the Presence (1 Kings 8:10,11; 2 Chronicles 5:13,14). At the giving of the law to Moses, Mount Sinai blazed with fire and smoke as God descended to meet with Moses. Fences and barriers held back the people for their own protection.

Whatever it means to enter God's presence, we must never forget that it is *God's* presence we enter. The God of Sinai, the temple, and the throne of heaven is in our midst when we worship whether He is visible (as in these accounts) or not. If we sat in church next Sunday and God suddenly drew back the veil to show us His glory that had gone unseen for countless weeks, people who would never bow their heads would instinctively prostrate themselves on the floor.

A Place for Awe and Silence

The frantic, demonic pace of our culture seems perfectly suited for the steady, yet often unnoticed, disintegration of human beings. Long hours on the job and extensive family obligations leave the little time remaining filled with exhaustion. Most of us in this shape aren't likely candidates to be smitten with awe of any kind because of the numbness that enshrouds our days like fog. But a capacity for awe must be cultivated if we are to worship God. Awe takes time and a heavy investment in a particular kind of energy. Knowing God will always elude those who want truth from God in a sound bite or have no time for spadework of the soul, but immediately press to the bottom line.

The Bible provides a key to unlock awe for people worn dull in their days. It lies within a single word: Behold! We don't use the word much in daily conversation and skip over it in Scripture. To behold means to look, but much more: to observe carefully, to drink in with our eyes until we perceive the real nature of what we behold. I am beholding when I do nothing but sit on my front steps and admire the crab apple blossoms on our tree. People heading for the expressway or rushing for the tennis courts three blocks away are too intent on other things to notice. Awe appropriately rises in the spirit when we drink in, or behold, beauty or grandeur—especially focusing on God, who stands behind His creation as its author.

We know this cultivating of awe in God's presence is growing inside us when we make friends with solitude and silence. Solitude does not mean just being alone, though cultivating awe starts there. We will never savor in awe the presence of God as long as we must have the presence of other people.

Our legitimate need for others lies ensconced in illegitimate parts of the heart. Sometimes we cannot cope with loneliness and must have a person to fill it. Often our esteem needs to "have" someone or else we cannot accept ourselves as persons. Relationships become idolatrous clutter that must be cleared away once they take root where only intimacy with God was meant to grow. As God is omnipresent (present in all places at all times), no one is ever genuinely alone. Solitude means being alone with God.

The Endangered Species

Silence is an endangered species. To those whose days are paneled with noise, silence positively roars, quickly intimidating us. For silence to exist, we must be quiet. Much of our walk with God lacks depth and we are often dull to His glory because we spend most of our time talking about Him and at Him. The substance of too much of our praying is telling God what we want and then leaving before He can say anything in reply.

Talking is one way we focus attention on ourselves. We must be heard; we must be listened to. Even in our worship, we're comfortable as long as there is sound—singing, reading, instrumental music, preaching, etc. We talk about flow and movement in worship, which often translates as no gaps, no lags, no silences where something otherwise might be going on.

No dead silence. But in truth, silence need not be dead; it can be pregnant with the presence of God. Beholding God in His majesty and glory should reduce us to silence. Entering God's presence, words become superfluous and even sinful intrusions as our descriptions and opinions carry the weight and import of dead leaves before the whirlwind.

> The Lord is in His holy temple. Let all the earth be silent before Him (Habakkuk 2:20).

> Be silent, all flesh, before the Lord; for He is aroused from His holy habitation (Zechariah 2:13).

In silence before God something else will happen. Peter, James, and John went with Jesus to a mountaintop one day, when suddenly not only was Jesus transformed by the visible glory of God but Moses and Elijah appeared and spoke with Him (Luke 9:29-36; see also Matthew 17:1-8; Mark 9:2-8). In the middle of things Peter began jabbering about tabernacles, not having a clue as to how to respond. So he reacted as he always did—by blustering in with words. A voice spoke out of the cloud of God's glory saying, "This is My Son, My Chosen One; listen to Him!" (Luke 9:35).

In silence before God, we can begin to learn to listen to Him. For most of us, listening is nothing more than enduring the contributions or heart sharing of others while our own words sit poised on our tongue like a burning cinder waiting to shoot forth. We must disengage all of our own agendas to concentrate on a singular agenda. Not only do we need to disengage our own agendas, but we need to drop the pressing stuff of the day that yips at our heels like bloodhounds.

> Guard your steps as you go to the house of God, and draw near to listen rather than to offer the sacrifice of fools; for they do not know they are doing evil. Do not be hasty in word or impulsive in thought to bring up a matter in the presence of God. For God is in heaven and you are on the earth; therefore let your words be few (Ecclesiastes 5:1,2).

God's majesty breaks us in that only what God has to say is genuinely important. We must be silent to begin to hear it.

A Place to Tremble

My landlord in college worked for the electric company. He specialized in repairing the high-tension power cables transporting electricity between cities. As we talked one day, I remarked how dangerous his job sounded. He replied, "As long as you don't forget what you're handling, everything's fine."

Awe and majesty should breed something deeper in the heart of those who know God through Jesus Christ—something tragically missing in much of what passes for Christian worship. The closest thing to a biblical fear of God that many of us can muster is habitual distant respect. But God is no tame, benign presence. The Scripture narratives in the last section underscore that vividly. So do these verses that seem quite alien to our Christian experience:

> The fear of the Lord is the beginning of knowledge; fools despise wisdom and instruction (Proverbs 1:7).

> Who would not fear Thee, O King of the nations: Indeed it is Thy due! For among all the wise men of the nations, and in all their kingdoms, there is none like Thee (Jeremiah 10:7).

These don't stand as isolated verses but as selections from an extensive variety of Scripture woven through the books of the Bible. We can't pile up bricks between the Testaments as if a biblical fear of God were part of Old Testament baggage we are now free to jettison. Note the teaching of Jesus and the life of the early church.

> I say to you, My friends, do not be afraid of those who kill the body, and after that have no more that they can do. But I will warn you whom to fear: fear the One who after He has killed has authority to cast into hell; yes, I tell you, fear Him! (Luke 12:4,5).

> So the church throughout all Judea and Galilee and Samaria enjoyed peace, being built up; and, going on in the fear of the Lord and in the comfort of the Holy Spirit, it continued to increase (Acts 9:31).

> It is a terrifying thing to fall into the hands of the living God (Hebrews 10:31).

This is no craven fear that drives us to run and hide from God but a marveling that we inhabit His presence and live—a hush and tiptoe born of keen awareness of where we stand. Roman Catholics are taught to apprehend the "mysterium tremendum" (the mysterious and awesome presence of God). Maybe they have something. As we sit discussing recipes and ball games before worship and talk to each other all through the service, can we make any legitimate claim to understanding that we are in the presence of God?

To embrace God is to reach out to a pillar of living, holy fire. To approach Him in awe and holy fear shows that we see clearly.

> Therefore, since we receive a kingdom which cannot be shaken, let us show gratitude,

by which we may offer to God an acceptable service with reverence and awe; for our God is a consuming fire (Hebrews 12:28,29).

It is the feeling of Isaiah's "undoneness" that places us on the doorstep of grace.

Dancing in the Fire

Israel stood assembled behind fences and barriers waiting. God, their deliverer from Egypt, was to come down; Mount Sinai would be His platform. The barriers insured that no one would get too near the mountain and perish. But Moses was an exception. Not only could he cross the barriers and approach the mountain where God would speak with him, but Moses could actually climb up into the cloud covering the mountain where God dwelt.

Grace is astounding; it is mercy given freely when only judgment is required. Grace's very nature humbles and breaks its recipients because, in light of both the holy nature of God and our own rebellious self-centeredness, it is so undeserved. Grace is never mere indulgence, a getting off the hook. Grace describes God becoming man to die to satisfy the penalty His law demands so He can offer forgiveness to the guilty. Grace is precious because an awesome God, one to be feared, purchased it at unimaginable cost to Himself.

Our shame runs deep in that many Christians live as if grace were something they were entitled to. No one has an inherent right to mercy; forgiveness is always a gift—an undeserved gift. Grace means that Moses can climb where he and others would normally have died in judgment. It means we can dance in the fire of God's presence without being consumed.

God's grace makes us bold on at least three fronts. Because my relationship with God rests on His grace through Jesus Christ, my failures do not destroy the relationship. I can live deeply secure in His love and grace amidst an insecure, performance-based world.

Grace also enlarges my heart for the things God would have me do. Great love evokes a great response in the beloved. This gives us a nutshell account of the motives of the apostles: They loved Jesus in response to His first loving them. Referring to his preaching the gospel, Paul said, ". . . of which I was made a minister, according to the gift of God's grace which was given to me according to the working of His power" (Ephesians 3:7). For those we love with all our heart, we will sacrifice and dare far beyond what we would do for ourselves. The apostles would have done anything for Jesus. For God to enlist us in anything He does is privilege beyond words.

Finally, grace allows me the freedom to fail and still grow. While I never want to fail, I still do at times. If perfection were the standard, I would be paralyzed with failure. Grace means God is pleased when, as His child, all I can do is toddle. Parents of infants go wild over their children's first attempts to speak. Gibbering and drooling, the child gurgles out some unintelligible mishmash and the father says, "Did you hear that? He said 'Daddy'!"

Our family worshiped one Sunday with an inner-city church in Chicago. At one point the worship leader asked us to divide into impromptu small groups for prayer. My son, possibly 11 years old, and I joined three people visiting from a charismatic church somewhere in Indiana. I wondered how Steve would handle this, as he hadn't done much public praying. A lot of us struggle with praying in public. Sometimes we fear saying something inappropriate that might be dishonoring to God. Most of the time we just don't want to embarrass ourselves.

We started praying around the little circle starting with our three new friends. Then it came to Steve.

"Father, I just . . . well, uh, I just . . . bless You," he muttered. The "sss" on "bless" was barely out of his mouth when the charismatics erupted.

"Yes, Jesus! Hear him, Lord! Glory to Your Name!" I could see in my son's eyes that he got the message: "I did okay and I didn't break anything important to God." So he went on.

"Lord, I just praise You because . . . uh, because You're good." Another volley from the charismatics from Indiana.

"That's right, Lord! Bless this boy! Praise You for Your goodness!" I never got to pray. Steve and his three new brothers rode out the rest of the prayer time. Charismatics can affirm prayer out of a fencepost. Steve's prayer life has grown since then, but it might never have happened if God hadn't bestowed grace to risk failure through three charismatics from Indiana. And with Steve's first mumbled attempt, I can see God cock His ear and say to a nearby angel, "Did you hear that? He said 'Father'!"

Grace means humbly knowing I stand when I should be consumed. Not only do I stand, but I dance and rejoice.

Breathing Air from Heaven

The Sunday-lunch-shift waiters at many restaurants all say the same thing: Christians can be lousy tippers. We want top service but sometimes show little appreciation for it. Our worship reflects the same at times; we treat praise as a gratuity. God will get it when He does something to deserve it. But Scripture reinforces the fact that there is never a time when God is not worthy of all our praise. To rejoice and revel in God's presence when we should be consumed cannot help but release our praise and adoration. It shouldn't have to be pried out of us, as C. S. Lewis points out.

> I had never noticed that all enjoyment spontaneously overflows into praise unless (sometimes even if) shyness or the fear of boring others is deliberately brought in to check it. . . . I had not noticed either that just as men spontaneously praise whatever they value, so they spontaneously urge us to join them in praising it: "Isn't she lovely? Wasn't it glorious? Don't you think that magnificent?" The

psalmists in telling everyone to praise God are doing what all men do when they speak of what they care about.[13]

Praise and adoration stand as the purest worship the human heart can render. Never are we more oblivious to our clamoring selves than when we praise God. The holy passion and even abandonment that sizzles through some of the psalms might embarrass us today. Adoration hones razor-sharp the deep appetites for God that we so easily stifle.

> One thing I have asked from the Lord, that I shall seek: that I may dwell in the house of the Lord all the days of my life, to behold the beauty of the Lord, and to meditate in His temple (Psalm 27:4).

> My soul longed and even yearned for the courts of the Lord; my heart and my flesh sing for joy to the living God (Psalm 84:2).

> As the deer pants for the water brooks, so my soul pants for Thee, O God. My soul thirsts for God, for the living God; when shall I come and appear before God? My tears have been my food day and night, while they say to me all day long, "Where is your God?" (Psalm 42:1-3).

Fog in the Sun?

The pressures, pain, and hassle that drag us down, the sin that repeatedly trips us up, and our inordinate desire for the good opinions of other people last as long as fog in brilliant morning sun when we worship and praise with a heart like the psalmist's. We strike fiercely at the deepest roots of deadness in our soul and refine with fire the coarsest jewels God has placed within us.

Praise and adoration, along with awe, majesty, and fear, all resonate best from within the spirits of broken people. They see with single eyes what the casually religious miss. Their thirsts and hungers go unquenched in the face of things most people would rather have to fill their hearts and lives. The God of majesty, awe, and grace breeds healthy and holy disgust for all pretenses of worship, of being Christian, that leave our own selfishness untouched at life's center.

Something rings exquisitely true about being swallowed up in adoration of the living God; it suits our spirit as a fitted glove to the hand. It reverberates with the natural rhythm of something we were created for. Nothing more pure can rise out of the heart of a Christian. Nothing more galvanizes the spirit in the face of trial and in the midst of daily life. Nothing more catalyzes our vision for serving amidst broken and hurting people (see Psalm 63:1-8).

True adoration is like the eclipse that comes when we fall under the shadow cast by the glory of God's presence. We are the temple that He longs to fill with all of Himself, with all His glory. What a cheap exchange we make to hoard even one dark corner of our lives for ourselves!

11

The Great Satisfaction

Much of the world's agenda centers around survival. Thousands of people died of starvation while we slept last night. The poor not only beg but sell vital organs or eyes for food. The street children of many Third World cities not only fall victim to prostitution and substance abuse but risk the horror of abduction, where profiteers harvest all body parts and organs for black market sale to medical schools and research labs. As I write, war shreds places like Somalia, the Middle East, and the provinces of what used to be Yugoslavia. Political and economic strife make the fragile freedom of the former Soviet Union highly negotiable.

By contrast, North Americans have made wholeness a multibillion-dollar industry. We juggle nutrition, exercise, meditation, self-help books, 12-step groups, and counseling therapies to correct deficiencies and to reverse neglect, to heal scars and generally improve a quality of life which often already is very good. We place all this under the banner of wholeness.

There's nothing wrong with wanting a healthy body or a sound mind, but our preoccupation with much of it testifies to how slippery wholeness can be. The harder we press for feeling good about ourselves, the more elusive it can be. Some things perpetually evaporate just outside our grasp; they were never meant to be goals but valuable by-products emerging as we strive for other things. Some things elude us because they're good things that have come to mean too much; they were never meant to be gods in our lives.

Knowing Jesus Christ should make a difference in our daily lives. In the Gospels we see people physically healed and released from demonic control. The average church has people bristling with opportunities both to transform and to be transformed. But neither may happen if we don't settle a crucial question at the root of our walk with God.

The life of the average Christian slides into the back-waters of mediocrity because, for various reasons, we don't recognize the times when issues that shape our lives are decided. Sometimes we're swallowed by things breaking loose or that scream for attention now. Sometimes we're muddle-headed and dull. But these decisive times rise quietly and obscurely, and our response in subtle, seemingly insignificant ways may shape our lives far more than the frantic concern of the moment thrust into our face.

The serious question we must settle involves the disposition of our heart toward Jesus Christ. Are we, as Christians, here to serve Him as Lord in the eyes of a dying world, or are we here to indulgently sit back expecting Him to wait on us?

Is This the Church or the Mall?

Both traditional American church experience and popular culture collaborate in making us people who often, even with the best intentions, are primarily Christian for what we get out of it. American church experience pre-conditions us that churches should not expect much of members. Expectations (and many Christians would find that word offensive) easily slip to the lowest common element. Ignoring the biblical teaching that the Holy Spirit carefully oversees and orchestrates the makeup of the Body of Christ (hence the local church; see 1 Corinthians 12:11-13), many Americans traditionally regard the church as an organization rather than an organism.

I can join wherever I like (without regard for where the Spirit of God may want to invest my gifts interfaced with the spiritual gifts of others) for whatever reasons. The church has no intrinsic claim on me and therefore no genuine ground for exacting any claim on me for involvement or any right to interfere with my life outside the morning worship service. I am doing the church a favor by joining. If I attend somewhat regularly, I am doing my part.

Sometimes we don't even have to attend. Any church that attempts to thin out the church rolls will surely bump into people unseen for years yet outraged at the thought of being dropped from the membership roll. The church of Jesus Christ is supposed to be there for us regardless of our minimal or nonexistent involvement; we may feel little or no reciprocal obligation to be there for Christ's church. If church-growth people figure rightly, these attenders may comprise as high as 75 percent of some church memberships. But things run deeper than this.

The sinful self-centeredness that would surely have slain us spiritually but for Christ dogs us right into the inner sanctum of our souls if we allow it to. As opposed to biblical worship, a worship service can cheapen into a trade floor where those who really have nothing to bargain with attempt to strike deals with the One who is holy and above all manipulation. "God, I'll come to church if . . ." People who have worked hard all their lives develop welfare mentalities toward God. We come to Him when He can do something for us, but for nothing else. If we attend church, it's God's part of the deal to provide, protect, bless, and heal for me and mine.

A little girl, after months of Wednesday nights in a prayer group of Christians, commented insightfully to her mother, "These people only want God when they're sick." The end result of this culminates in people asking God for blessing to undergird nice, respectable, nominally Christian but functionally secular lives. But God never pours out grace to indulge atrophy and spiritual anesthesia; He lavishes His grace to forgive, cleanse, and raise us to a level of magnificence that only He can bring forth.

Sometimes the church is an accomplice to this. In our theology and outreach, we give license to this "get" mentality. The popularity of "prosperity teaching," which basically promises that God wants all Christians to be materially wealthy, inflates materialistic hopes that Jesus never intended to raise—hopes that burst like balloons and leave people devastated both spiritually and monetarily.

I remember attending a service one night where this message was heard all the time. Many of the attendees were friends of mine, people whom life had treated harshly, people who knew the bitter taste of financial hardship. Here they stood dressed in the only clothes they had, not designer clothes but better than I had seen them wear on the street. We stood and joined hands to close in prayer. The pastor led and asked those present to repeat after him.

"I am a winner! God wants me to prosper . . . in every way . . . every day! I will overcome! I claim my riches now!"

This wasn't prayer but a mantra that people chanted under the pretense of prayer to convince themselves of its truth. I saw hopes burning hot and deep like flames flickering deep inside an oil lamp. Months later the flames were snuffed out as the church imploded, leaving people whom Jesus loved strewn in the debris like discarded rag dolls. Jesus never lured people with money, never enticed people with the things that were killing them. That's why He didn't promise the rich young ruler any kind of payoff on this planet and refused to taint His teaching by touching a dime of what the young man was told to give away (Matthew 19:16-22).

Striking a Deal?

Our methods could stand probing as well. We are a nation of consumers looking to strike the best deal we can get. Advertisers know how to play off our felt needs and even how to create a sense of need where there isn't one. The mall is the shrine where all the "want" and "felt need" options anyone could want fit under one roof. Shopping is recreation. Spending now mushrooms as one of the most rapidly growing compulsions we indulge in to compensate for any number of inadequacies, real or imagined. Whatever our motivation to frequent the marketplace, our eyes wax hot and eager for what we want at as low a cost as possible.

Churches that mount an impressive array of ministries stand as wonderful examples of what churches can do when determined to maximize their gifts and other resources. But is it biblical to expect new buildings, expanded parking lots, Saturday night services, worship bands playing Scripture choruses, support groups for everything imaginable, beautiful sanctuaries, altar flowers, drama, five-star youth programs, and a sparkling professional staff to draw people in?

One pastor stood in a meeting proclaiming, "We have bowling alleys, a day-care, a full gymnasium, and ample parking. Who wouldn't want to go to our church?" Another pastor sadly related how many of his church members had left to go to the megachurch nearby. Some were close friends and longtime members of the board. Had a church fight splintered this fellowship? No, the pastor says he simply was outpreached; the people left to listen to the nationally renowned preacher at the large church. Places of ministry were deserted without notice. Some people left without so much as a goodbye or an explanation for their friend, the pastor.

The strategy of the early church consisted of nothing else than lives being made holy and Christlike, joyfully penetrating the darkness around them. Programs, events, and personalities have their place, but nothing substitutes for God's Spirit radiating Jesus Christ in holiness and power through frail, common human personalities. We place our primary messianic hopes on programs, expansion, and gimmicks. The average church outreach committee will ask, "What can we do to get people in?" The used car dealer down the road from us wonders the same.

Questions on whether we are in heart what we ought to be in Christ seldom surface. It is far more comfortable discussing and engineering the fund-raising for a new four-million-dollar church complex than to probe the cost of being filled with the Holy Spirit of God. (Maybe we intrinsically understand that it costs far less to erect a four-million-dollar edifice than to be filled with God's Spirit.) To juggle programs and structure and to provide the widest array of services without the reality of Jesus Christ does nothing more than provide a religious mall. The people may indeed come, but only until another church nearby tops us and draws them away.

The epidemic church-hopping of Americans provides tragic proof that our stance toward God undergirded by traditional low expectations, poor theology, and treating people as consumers is too often the attitude of being in it for what we can get out of it.

Check the Blueprints

I stood by the window watching the forms go up. Then the cement truck arrived and began to pour what would be the walls of an addition of much-needed ministry space. But something didn't look right after everything was poured. A flight of steps should have run up one outside corner, but I didn't see them. When the builders returned, I asked about it and they assured me everything was fine—until they checked the blueprints. The flight of steps had been omitted when the walls were formed up. The builders had to cut out a ten-foot length of concrete wall six inches thick to correct the oversight.

God has placed in Scripture ample design of the different rhythms and nuances of knowing Him. For example, is it wrong to come to God asking for things—help, provision, protection, health, etc.? Can we come too often? Does God ever get fed up with our constant coming and then shut off His blessing? Of course not.

> Give us this day our daily bread. And forgive us our debts, as we also have forgiven our debtors. And do not lead us into temptation, but deliver us from evil (Matthew 6:11-13).

> What man is there among you, when his son shall ask him for a loaf, will give him a stone? Or if he shall ask for a fish, he will not give him a snake, will he? If you then, being evil, know how to give good gifts to your children, how much more shall your Father who is in heaven give what is good to those who ask Him! (Matthew 7:9-11).

God's capacity to give infinitely exceeds our capacity to receive. But the fatal misdirection we have taken is to lock in on God being primarily a giver and ourselves as primarily receivers.

What does the blueprint say? What did God intend to evoke from human lives touched by Christ? What is the church here for? How can my life mean something, and do I have to strive for it only to fall unfulfilled? Scripture says that something incredible is in process in the life of every Christian. The blueprint says we are to be conformed to the image of Jesus Christ.

> Whom He foreknew, He also predestined to become conformed to the image of His Son,

that He might be the firstborn among many brethren (Romans 8:29).

> ... always carrying about in the body the dying of Jesus, that the life of Jesus also may be manifested in our body. For we who live are constantly being delivered over to death for Jesus' sake, that the life of Jesus also may be manifested in our mortal flesh (2 Corinthians 4:10,11).

The indwelling Holy Spirit works throughout our earthly Christian lives to refine, purge, and cleanse us with the end in mind that Jesus Christ literally lives His life through us. As He does so, our lives become transformed as they take on more and more of His nature while preserving our own uniqueness. Top priority on the blueprint is that God through the Holy Spirit will work in every Christian until he or she is like Jesus. While this won't be complete until we get to heaven (1 John 3:2), He will settle for no substitutes, nothing less.

Looking at Jesus

If Jesus is the prototype of what God wants to make us, His life is worth a hard look. Was Jesus primarily concerned with what He was getting from God or with how passionately He could serve God? Listen to this part of the blueprint.

> Think of yourselves the way Christ Jesus thought of himself. He had equal status with God but didn't think so much of himself that he had to cling to the advantages of that status no matter what. Not at all. When the time came, he set aside the privileges of deity and took on the status of a slave, became _human!_ Having become human, he stayed human. It was an incredibly humbling process. He didn't

claim special privileges. Instead, he lived a selfless, obedient life and then died a selfless, obedient death—and the worst kind of death at that; a crucifixion.[14]

Jesus plunged into the shatteredness of human affairs holding nothing back. He took the worst with His eyes open and knowing it was coming. He didn't negotiate how much privilege He could keep and still do God's will.

What else does the blueprint say? John writes poignantly of the disciples' last night together with Jesus before His crucifixion. Jesus did and said many memorable things that night. One particularly etched itself in their minds and hearts in a humbling way. The 12 disciples repeatedly squabbled over which of them was the greatest. That night Jesus decisively skewered their presumption and pomposity without a word. He simply rose from the table after supper and stripped down like a common servant. Then, over protestations particularly from Peter, He washed their feet when their pride forbade them to do this for one another (John 13:1-11). Then Jesus underscored the point.

> If I then, the Lord and the Teacher, washed your feet, you also ought to wash one another's feet. For I gave you an example that you also should do as I did to you. Truly, truly, I say to you, a slave is not greater than his master; neither is one who is sent greater than the one who sent him. If you know these things, you are blessed if you do them (John 13:14-17).

Jesus knew of their and our tendencies to fight tooth and nail over shabby little kingdoms that fly our own drooping flags. But in the greatness God acknowledges, there is magnificence in the humblest task. He who sharpens a pencil or scrubs a toilet for the kingdom of God may be making a more powerful contribution toward eternity than a CEO from General Motors. Jesus had already taught as much when He said, "The Son of Man did not come to be served, but to serve, and to give His life a ransom for many" (Matthew 20:28).

If we are conformed to the image of Jesus Christ—this Jesus—what contentment can God then find in our love affair with the status quo in church life? Can we still masquerade our unwillingness to cross the barriers of comfort and convenience with a self-interest that would almost rather go to hell than not get its own way?

God's blueprint for the different facets of knowing Him includes far more than just what God wants to make of us. Deep hungers, legitimate ones, well up from deep within us all. Apart from Jesus Christ we are highly likely to misspend, squander, or destroy our precious lives in trying to satisfy real hungers with rags and scraps. How can I find real meaning and purpose that doesn't wash away like sand with the tide? Jesus pulls back another page of God's blueprints when He says:

> If you don't go all the way with me, through thick and thin, you don't deserve me. If your first concern is to look after yourself, you'll never find yourself. But if you forget about yourself and look to me, you'll find both yourself and me.[15]

> Self-help is no help at all. Self-sacrifice is the way, my way, to finding yourself, your true self. What kind of deal is it to get everything you want but lose yourself?[16]

Swallowed in Service

Meaning and purpose come not by clutching and clawing for it but by complete abandonment to Jesus Christ and allowing our lives to be swallowed up in serving Him. Mary is a special friend whose life rises like cream above many. The doctors knew something wasn't right when, by the age of four, Mary's vocabulary included no more than six words. Looking back, Mary's mother remembered that an hour-and-a-half before Mary's birth the mother received an injection of something. Whatever the medication was, it caused Mary's mother to lose her sight for three days and certainly entered the baby's system, possibly causing neurological impairment. Now, 36 years later, Mary lives with her parents.

People who know her testify to her radiant smile, sharp sense of humor, and childlike faith. Mary knits and crochets. Casual onlookers might say it's nice she has something like that to fill her time. But Mary's handiwork is no patronizing time-filler. In one year she knit over 120 long, thick scarves and gave them to the Salvation Army to give to the poor at Christmas.

Then one day Mary saw a news broadcast describing the predicament of the homeless in winter. Two men interviewed refused shelter, preferring to sleep under the highway overpasses. "Just give us blankets," they said. One of them died of exposure that very night. Mary couldn't get that out of her mind. The picture of that man's face burned in her heart like a hot cinder. She started to throw herself into making even more scarves until her mother pointed out that scarves couldn't warm a person's whole body and suggested that Mary make afghans instead. Now Mary's ministry to the needy consists of averaging 80 or more afghans a year—many big enough to cover a double bed.

The early Christians in the city of Joppa included a woman named Dorcas who may never have preached or taught but put the love of Jesus into every stitch of everything she made (Acts 9:36-42). No one may ever get to thank Mary personally for their scarf or afghan; Mary doesn't knit or crochet to be thanked. But a thanks is coming. Jesus said, "I was . . . naked and you clothed Me. . . . To the extent that you did it to one of these brothers of Mine, even the least of them, you did it to Me" (Matthew

25:35,36,40). When Mary enters Jesus' presence, He may well welcome her wrapped up in something she will recognize.

Mary doesn't have time or inclination to think about how she feels about herself or whether she is happy and fulfilled. Many of us who are healthy in body and mind but whose spirit is sick, self-centered, and empty cannot say the same. Meaning and purpose? It is provided for in the blueprints, and Jesus is fashioning Mary right down to the specifications—if her parents don't land in the poorhouse trying to keep her in yarn!

Crushed by the Load?

Many people have little time to think about what God wants to do in them or to work through their deepest hungers. They're pulverized under crushing loads of worry about how they're going to survive. The blueprint has something for them too.

> Instead of looking at the fashions, walk out into the fields and look at the wildflowers. They never primp or shop, but have you ever seen color and design quite like it? The ten best-dressed men and women in the country look shabby alongside them.
>
> If God gives such attention to the appearance of wildflowers—most of which are never even seen—don't you think he'll attend to you, take pride in you, do his best for you? What I'm trying to do here is to get you to relax, to not be so preoccupied with *getting*, so you can respond to God's *giving*. People who don't know God and the way he works fuss over these things, but you know both God and how he works. Steep your life in God-reality, God-initiative, God-provisions. Don't worry about

missing out. You'll find all your everyday human concerns will be met.

Give your entire attention to what God is doing right now, and don't get worked up about what may or may not happen tomorrow. God will help you deal with whatever hard things come up when the time comes.[17]

Serving doesn't happen in our spare time. It's an attitude permeating every area of life right in the middle of where we are. When we voluntarily choose to give up our preoccupation with what we're getting out of our walk with God and instead throw ourselves into serving Him and others, all that we've needed and desired, as well as more than we can imagine, will sprout faster than spring wildflowers.

The blueprint for the church is the same. We are to stand as salt (Matthew 5:13), living holy lives in the middle of a dying world, lives that vibrate with life. We are to be light (Matthew 5:14-16), impossible to miss and making our Savior impossible to miss as well. He never pours out His Holy Spirit on anyone to hoard or boast over but to be witnesses to Him (Acts 1:8).

Jesus never wanted Christians to build buildings and sit in them with that same dead self-satisfaction that characterized the Pharisees. He told us instead to go out into all the world (Matthew 28:19,20). To serve lost humanity in the midst of terrible darkness is the only reason Christ left us on the earth. When we refuse to do this because of our preoccupation with getting God to anoint our own agendas, we make our Lord look shabby in the eyes of those who need Him most.

12

Giving My Life Away

When we lay all concern of cost on the shelf to assume the life of a servant of Jesus, we become the freest person imaginable. Things we once longed to have now drop from us like rusty locks hammered off by God. Once these may have been precious, and maybe they still mean more than they should, but even though it may sting, Jesus liberates His servants from at least five mind-sets.

Focusing on giving our lives away instead of on our own fulfillment frees us first of all from the need to be treated well. Servants aren't pampered. In some parts of the world, being a spiritual leader means persecution; in America it often means privilege with perks comparable to that of a CEO. With our conferences and seminars aping those in the business world, that fact should come as no surprise.

Many churches strike unspoken deals with pastoral staffs in which the church pays the staff well to do the ministry while the church sits back like patrons. But it is the consumer, the customer, who feels entitled to being treated well in this world. We often entertain attitudes of privilege that grow out of our supposed status. Monetary giving, a family name respected in the community, tenure in the church, or having an ordination certificate can cause us to imagine we're something we're not.

When my credit card bill came in the mail, I winced. Somehow a 200-dollar purchase of books showed up. While I'm capable of coveting that many books at one time, I did not make the purchase and dreaded the hassle of getting it removed from my account. I phoned the bookseller first, hoping to avoid going to the bank. The customer service lady eased my mind right away. She found the mistake and would set things straight with the bank.

I was ready to hang up when the woman came back on the line. "I want to thank you," she said, "for being so understanding about this. I'm a fairly new Christian and I thought it would be great working for a Christian bookseller. We deal with pastors, missionaries, and all kinds of Christian leaders, and you wouldn't believe how we're treated when their orders aren't handled exactly right."

Unruffling Our Feathers

A servant has no right to pampered or privileged treatment. While it's nice, needing or expecting it makes us soft and spiritually self-indulgent. Jesus never promised His servants that they would be treated well by a world that crucified Him. If we weren't so full of ourselves, we wouldn't get our feathers ruffled so easily. Instead of being upset when we're being treated poorly, maybe we should praise God. Jesus Himself might be doing it to knock some pomposity and pretense out of us. The world that treats us less than well is paying us a compliment. Peter wrote, "If you are reviled for the name of Christ, you are blessed" (1 Peter 4:14). They're telling us that we have unknowingly been embracing God in Jesus Christ tight enough for some of Him to rub off.

The life that lifts serving over getting is also free from needing to get the credit or to see results. Achievement stands as one of the most satisfying feelings I know, but life does not always reward us with that sense of accomplishment and the accompanying credit that comes with it. The standard that Jesus posts for the one who serves is not results but faithfulness—staying with it even if results aren't readily apparent (1 Corinthians 4:1,2).

In a society devoted to instant gratification, we don't wait very long to see things happen. God works in His perfect time which makes no allowance for our impatience. He works where we do not see. He works through people unknown to us.

Even if we do not see results when we would like, that does not mean they are not coming. William Carey, the great missionary to India, went six years before seeing his first convert. Mission agencies that might not look favorably on similar performance in their people today recognize Carey as the father of modern world missions. Paul wrote, "Let us not lose heart in doing good, for in due time we shall reap if we do not grow weary" (Galatians 6:9). When the results do finally come to light, their magnitude will always require the praise of His glory (Ephesians 1:6,12,14).

To serve rather than to freeload on God's dole liberates us from needing the good opinion of others; a servant must only please his master. We all like to be liked, and all of us know the weight and stress of living under expectations that conflict or are excessive. The old adage about not being able to please everyone doesn't stop us from trying. Serving Jesus lifts us from trying to satisfy the clamor of human demands by fine-tuning us until we desire to please only Him. Serving Jesus is not drudgery but joy.

> Come to Me, all who are weary and heavy-laden, and I will give you rest. Take My yoke upon you, and learn from Me, for I am gentle and humble in heart; and you shall find rest for

your souls. For My yoke is easy, and My load is light (Matthew 11:28-30).

Well Done!

This summer I went with 11 of our youth to the woods of upstate Michigan. We worked to start a new church and to shore up the ministry of a wounded church in two different towns. We had prayed and trained for months and put in 12-hour days. God did incredible things that week, and 11 young people saw the Holy Spirit do through them what only God could do.

In our last evening together, as we prayed, I saw Jesus speak His "well done" to their hearts. It happened simultaneously; they all heard it and wept. The "well done" of the Master is all the one serving needs to hear; there's nothing like it.

Jesus' "well done" also galvanizes us to cope with the slings and arrows of those we disappoint when we please Him. In pleasing the Father, Jesus was accused of being demonized. The Roman governor told Paul he was insane. Sad to say, any Christian who serves Jesus determined to hear only His "well done" may feel the sting of criticism from family and other Christians. When that happens, it is only a reminder of who we really need to please—not others, and not ourselves, but the One who dignified our lives by calling us to serve Him.

When we throw our lives into serving Jesus, He marvelously liberates us from the need to be justified when misunderstood or falsely accused. Nothing in Scripture says we are to bend over backward to answer false accusations after a reasonable attempt to set things straight.

Our ego and wounded pride smolder with the memory of things said that we simply refuse to let go. We lie awake at night seething with anger and fantasizing scenarios where our critics get beaten and thoroughly humiliated. When we are misunderstood, slandered, or falsely accused, our best attempts to set things straight may fail. Some would rather believe the lie. The one who throws his life into serving lives not for self-vindication but for his Master. The Master will set things straight when it counts.

> You have been called for this purpose, since Christ also suffered for you, leaving you an example for you to follow in His steps. ... While being reviled, He did not revile in return; while suffering, He uttered no threats, but kept entrusting Himself to Him who judges righteously (1 Peter 2:21,23).

Cutting Loose

Cutting loose to serve Jesus liberates us from needing to be in control. Control is the most important issue in millions of lives today. We simply must dominate, must control, in our relationships, our work, our emotions, and even in church. Things must go our way; we must get our way. Pastors sometimes hesitate to delegate ministry because they fear losing control. Business meetings can become stages where the muscles of clout, manipulation, and even intimidation shamefully ripple.

The thing that galled the Pharisees most about Jesus was that they could not control Him. If God had anything to say to anyone, it would surely be to them. If God did anything, it would be in ways they had always recognized, approved of, and could control. But Jesus destroyed all their neat prescribed ideas of what God should be like.

Deep down, we don't fret and worry over things we can't control; we worry and fret that we can't control certain things. Jesus lifts all that from those who serve Him. A servant doesn't need to be in control, doesn't need to give orders. All the servant does is to obey the wishes of the Master. When we stiffen and begin to tell God what He ought to be like or what He ought to do, Jesus simply pushes through our stringent rules and carefully laid parameters.

Embracing God

Jesus is Lord; we control Him no more than a pup tent could cage a Bengal tiger. When was the last time Jesus Christ dropped our jaw both in amazement and in the humble acknowledgment that we don't understand Him nearly as well as we thought—certainly not well enough to control?

This liberating may really chafe at us because freedom is only attractive when it appears to be what we want. When we would rather be treated well and kept comfortable, always making sure to get our share of the spotlight, to make our mark, to have our good reputations on the tongues of others, to have our name kept clear at all costs, to always call the shots—then the freedom Jesus offers appears to be a threat.

But to take one step away from all this toward what Jesus offers is to taste something the world cannot give but can only attempt to counterfeit. I met a girl yesterday who spent her summer working in an inner-city center in Detroit amidst the worst heartbreak and squalor the city has. She said she signed up for two more years. I laughed and said, "Got into your blood, huh?"

"That's it," she grinned back. She's not in Detroit's Cass Corridor to save the world. But she has never felt the embrace of the One who will indeed save the world so tightly and warmly as she does down there. And now others in Detroit's inner city feel it too because she is there.

The Servant's Union Card

The Christian who throws himself into living this life of joyous abandonment through serving will see wholeness emerge in his life but will also discover that his or her pain is redeemed as well. Nobody likes pain. We avoid it whenever we can, shed it as soon as possible, and jettison the memory of it if we can. But our pain, the comfort we receive from God in the midst of it, and the brokenness that keeps us empty of self and full of Jesus make up our "union card," our right to enter lives in pain.

> Blessed be the God and Father of our Lord
> Jesus Christ, the Father of mercies and God of
> all comfort; who comforts us in all our afflic-
> tion so that we may be able to comfort those
> who are in any affliction with the comfort with
> which we ourselves are comforted by God
> (2 Corinthians 1:3,4).

Biographies reveal that many, if not most, of the people God has used throughout church history intimately knew pain in body and mind. Their pain never impeded Christ in His living vibrantly through them; indeed, Christ redeemed their pain and fashioned it into a key opening the hearts of many.

Many Christians use and are thankful for *Cruden's Concordance*. Alexander Cruden, the compiler, suffered from severe mental illness and spent three separate times in an insane asylum. He caused serious problems on his job (where he excelled as a proofreader) because he couldn't get along with anyone. He was finally fired, but Cruden refused to leave because he believed it was God's will that he be there.

Cruden also caused scenes at church, making his responses in a loud voice while gesturing wildly. He also appointed himself corrector of all morals, manners, and grammar in his town. He confronted people publicly over incidentals as well as sensitive indiscretions that should have been discussed privately. Some people were less than appreciative; brawls and fistfights broke out.

But for most of his tormented adult life, Alexander Cruden went every Sunday to London's vile Newgate Prison, where he preached Christ to the prisoners. The hardened inmates of Newgate looked to him as the father that many never really had. And many said that honey never dripped sweeter from the comb than grace from the lips of Alexander Cruden. He also spent much time and most of his meager funds interceding for prisoners with magistrates and prison officials.

The Healing Tools

Today all over the world nothing has changed. Common, ordinary people with pain and sickness become powerful healing tools. When we embrace God and His life surges through us, we can never be so caught up with Him that we forget those who have never felt so much as a touch, let alone an embrace.

Being Christ's not only means being broken in physical, mental, or spiritual pain in order to bring empathy to the lives of fragmented people. It also means sharing the pain of God's heart for the world. Christians speak of having a burden. A burden is nothing less than the Holy Spirit mediating some of the actual pain of God's heart for the lostness of man and the fallenness of all creation. To whatever degree, we are allowed to feel the wounded heart of the Father over man's alienation and rebellion. We feel His ravaged and lacerated holiness over the vileness and magnitude of individual and corporate sin. We feel it for friends and relatives and for entire nations such as South Africa and its racial strife.

We could not survive feeling the pain in God's heart at full strength, but one unmistakable mark of growing up lies in finding that God enlarges our heart and kindles our desire to ask Him to share even more of His pain with us. This is the spiritual plutonium that fuels intercessors.

Sharing this pain also sharpens vision like nothing else and detonates us into strategic action. Linda began to feel God's heartache for the poor in her Iowa hometown. Praying over this, she felt compelled to take some Christian literature down to the clinic where people came to sell their blood. One woman sat waiting but showed little interest or response in Linda's attempts to start a conversation. One or two subsequent visits brought the same response. But every time she walked into that clinic, Linda's heart broke a little more.

One day the Lord asked, "Linda, what kind of people sell their blood?" Linda knew: the poor and desperate.

They were hardly likely to trust anyone enough to open up if that other person wasn't in the same boat. So, over the protests of some who warned about health risks and how it would look, Linda started selling her blood at the clinic. And she began to make friends with single welfare mothers and prostitutes who frequented the clinic. And they began to meet Jesus. Linda, her husband, and their four kids could really have used the money she received, but the family gave it all to the Lord.

Linda had to finally slow down because she was getting sick from selling blood too often. Her husband joked that he couldn't afford all the Geritol it would take to pump her blood iron level back up! Linda maintained her new friendships, though, and more of these people felt the embrace of Jesus Christ. We moved away and I lost touch, but I can imagine her going right back as soon as her strength was up.

Flaming Nuggets of Pain

Much of what we refer to as a burden really isn't that at all. We get distressed over someone's problem or need or over some international crisis or ongoing situation. But our daily routines quickly pave over these twinges that may resurface later as a regretful "Oh, yes, I meant to pray about that" or "That's a shame" as we peruse the newspaper.

When God burdens a heart, placing His pain over a dying world in it as mediated through the Holy Spirit, it does not go away as long as the need exists. Quite the contrary—it burns like a nugget of flaming phosphorus growing hotter all the time. These flames are always specific, and manifest themselves in two primary ways.

They drive us to passionate prayer at all times of the day and night. Unrelenting intercessory prayer that bites down and won't let go (and has leveled kingdoms as well as vanguarding fiery spiritual awakening) flows like lava from the burdened heart.

Burdens also detonate us into action. The classic mystics have been badly misrepresented as people who locked themselves away in castle towers and monasteries praying all the time. Many of the great mystics knew fierce persecution, and some even martyrdom, for all the trouble they caused by forcing the kingdom of God into the marketplace and the palace.

Pressing deep with God is no excuse for hiding from the world. Christian discipleship junkies who hit every home Bible study and line their bookshelves with the discipling notebooks from all the seminars without spending on others the riches of Christ they have garnered are misdirected at best if not spiritually selfish. People of depth with God need no one to push them into action. Their lives lie with the quiet readiness of expertly crafted arrows waiting for God's sure eye and His strong arm and bow.

A woman I know here in Detroit grapples with this now. Gifted in working with very young children, she began to be pressed by the thought of "crack" babies— babies born with cocaine addictions due to the mother's drug use during pregnancy. Those substance-addicted babies filled more and more of her thoughts; they began to wake her up at night. Hours of lost sleep were swallowed in prayer.

As of now, she feels a pain so severe for them that praying isn't enough. She must do something and is banging on God's door quite hard to find out what. She can know no peace in her heart and life as long as newborn babies cry out for cocaine and heroin. God has married her heart to those tiny crying ones: She has a burden from God.

Scripture underscores the same kind of heartache in Jesus and Paul. In the last week of Jesus' life, with the fickle cheers of the crowd behind Him and betrayal, denial, and the cross to come, Jesus openly cried out in grief over the sin and judgment to fall on those about to kill Him (Matthew 23:37-39; Luke 13:34,35).

Our tendency is different. A pastor friend once said, "It's hard not to rejoice when your enemies take it in the neck." Paul wept over people whose sin made them enemies of Christ (Philippians 3:18) and honestly said that if his damnation could redeem his kinsmen, the Jews, he would gladly see his salvation renounced (Romans 9:1-3). Paul also carried all those infant churches all over the Mediterranean in his heart, feeling every struggle as if it were a knife twisting in his stomach (2 Corinthians 11:28,29).

The Yardstick of Our Tears

The tragedy and indictment of much that passes for Christianity in America today lies measured in the yardstick of our tears. Our tears are too often spent only along natural lines and relationships where pain infects our personal concerns. The hand of God stands poised over the church, over the person who will weep the tears and carry the pain of God. All the satisfactions, joy, meaning, and freedom that humans crave elude the fiercest pursuit. But they bloom richly with life of their own in those who see life in Christ as something more than just a primary way to obtain and embellish their wants and concerns.

The rich meaning and satisfaction found in serving Christ allures, but carrying the burden that fuels the serving can intimidate. People who willingly carry a burden from God stand apart from rank-and-file church members. They make others feel uncomfortable and guilty, and therefore sometimes angry. Jean Vanier, founder of the worldwide L'Arche Communities (Christian communities that exist solely to minister to the physically and mentally handicapped), puts it well.

> If someone receives a special call from Jesus and starts growing toward a greater love and compassion . . . there will come a moment when he or she begins to reveal the mediocrity of others and thus becomes dangerous. . . . They make people ask questions about their own mediocrity but they are unwilling to face them and seek change.[18]

Stop and think for a moment: How many people can be trusted with the deepest pain in our lives? When we bestow that trust on someone, we accord him or her a high privilege and pay a rich compliment. He is worthy of our trust. I sense this when a counselee divulges some deeply buried information that till then had been locked up tight. As God begins to shape us into His image and our hearts begin to ache like His, we dare not pull back. In this self-worshiping "me-first" world, how many of us can be trusted to share the deep pain in the heart of God? He simply cannot entrust a burden to just anyone. To receive such a burden is the highest trust imaginable.

One of the deepest and richest aspects of embracing God lies in embracing as our own those things that cause Him the most pain. It is not to be missed. Few people recognize the incredible honor. Fewer still are found worthy of the honor.

The burdens of God blaze only on the altars of those too abandoned to His kingdom to be preoccupied with what they are getting out of it. God Himself ensures they will get more than they dreamed possible. To the ones who will venture to carry His pain as if it were their own, God in Jesus Christ gives His richest treasure. To those who embrace Him, God gives all His heart.

13

Stretching the Spirit

Growing hurts. I remember lying in bed while my mother rubbed my legs to soothe the ache of a young body growing quickly. As a boy, baseball and music filled every empty nook and cranny of my life that things like school didn't demand. Jammed fingers, bruises, and hours squirreled away in practice seemed a small price to pay for the joy of a growing skill in things I loved. The later insecurities in peer and especially dating relationships, as well as the first big move away from home to college, all needed to be faced as part of maturing.

Growth sounds attractive; it means expansion, improvement, development, and vitality. Spiritual growth magnifies all these meanings many times over. The smallest spark of life in Christ makes us cry out for more. The desire to grow may lie frustrated or choked off for years; it can be run into the ground through self-inflicted spiritual dryness and neglect. But Christ's life in us through the Holy Spirit longs and strives to expand and control every fiber of our being, eclipsing all competitors for first claim on our lives.

Most Christians want to grow. To not care about growing evidences something seriously wrong with our spiritual lives. Who could authentically know even the smallest vestige of intimacy with Christ and not want more? But spiritual growth, like growth in any other area in life, comes at a price. All of us have cast wistful glances at what we would like to be, at behaviors we would like to see eradicated as well as life patterns we long to take on.

But good intentions aren't enough; we have logged plenty of false starts and failed attempts. While God's grace has enough elasticity to encompass all the failure we can compile in a lifetime, some of our failure was guaranteed because we either took growth for granted or expected it to be easy. Some people window-shop for Christlikeness, the fruit and fullness of the Holy Spirit, and holiness, only to move on to something less desirable but a little more affordable. But we needn't do so.

The launchpad of motivation for Christian growth lies solidly based on hungers (for holiness, for Christlikeness) that God awakens in the heart of Christians which compel us to stretch and to submit to things in ways we otherwise would not. It originates not in our frail good intentions or inconsistent follow-throughs. God Himself births the desire, the motivation, and the allurement of what only He can do.

For the promises of Christ's riches, we undertake and endure much that we would never submit to for our own concerns. In that context, allies and guides toward Christ's riches take on strange shapes. While growth in Christ will mean different things for many people (God is a creative innovator, not an impersonal mass producer; He treats people as individuals) but certainly the same basics for all, beyond the basics God may place disciplines and structure testing into one life that may mean little in another.

But one element common to every life (although the precise shape varies in each) is that major formative moments in our lives involve turning corners that are not smooth, confronting things we might avoid if possible but could not foresee. Christian growth redeems pain and apparent waste, utilizing things that challenge us beyond the walls of comfort and convenience. Going through those walls always breaks us, but only to knock loose the dryness and rigidity of death that, left to ourselves, slowly encrusts us all.

A brief look at a few of these may deliver us from the poisons of grumbling and complaint—low-grade but highly effective toxins of all the Holy Spirit's work, of all that God rejoices over in His work in the human soul. Such a look may also prime us for powerful surges of growth and accelerated usefulness under the hand of God. For those willing to pay the steeper price, God has even steeper rewards.

The Texture of Lordship

"Jesus is Lord!" We say it in a second. It takes a lifetime to learn. Familiarity may not always breed contempt; sometimes it breeds dullness. The primary threat to intimate relationships sustained over time lies in the creeping onset of taking the other for granted, blurring the lines of their identity. But both young Christians and seasoned believers stumble over the everyday implications of Jesus as Lord.

One facet of Christ's lordship difficult to handle is submission. Like castor oil, submission is something we choke down when we must. We begrudgingly render it to the government and our employers, but in the private spheres of our life, where the muscles of desire and will ripple and flex, we vehemently resist being told what to do by anybody. The only one I must please down deep inside is myself.

Submission challenges and confronts that. We're convinced that fulfillment comes only when we strive to free ourselves from the control of others. Submission to anyone suffocates freedom, authenticity, and fulfillment. Sad to say, many people who feel this way walk away from even the normal demands and obligations brought on by family responsibilities. "I no longer feel fulfilled. He or she can no longer make me happy. I feel constricted and trapped and must have my freedom."

A simple reading of any of the Gospels shows that Jesus is Lord. He freely accepted that name and title from the disciples (John 13:13). Quite simply, Jesus stands as more than a Savior; He is the boss. There is no time when I clock out of being a Christian the way we clock out of our jobs and out from under the authority of our supervisors. Jesus Christ does not forgive sin only to release us to live self-absorbed lives.

On the way to Jerusalem one day, Jesus encountered ten lepers who cried out to be healed. Jesus told them to go show themselves to the priest. As they went the leprosy vanished, and one, a Samaritan (spiritual half-breeds held in contempt by Jews) returned praising God and falling on his face in gratitude at Christ's feet. The other nine never looked back (Luke 17:11-18).

The Nine Ungrateful Lepers

The recovery movement, in both its Christian and secular expressions, is powerfully with us. Problems such as abuse of all kinds, substance addiction, sexual assault, depression, and dysfunctional families didn't just spring upon us in the last 30 years or so. These terrible problems have long plagued sinful people of every culture, although they have almost always been hushed up and ignored. Christian bookstores do well selling recovery titles, thereby testifying to how many people in the church carry scars and fresh wounds into the service every week.

In light of all this, those nine ungrateful lepers should disturb us more than they do. Does Jesus come just to heal the scars of our past or eradicate the dysfunction of our present, and nothing more? The Christian recovery movement sees many people rising above the adult aftermath of having alcoholic parents (and grappling with and over-coming the scars of abuse) only to go on to live morally respectable, self-indulgent, functionally secular lives. We pick up Jesus as a healing therapy that we stay with until we get clear of our mess and then move on.

Jesus is the Lord, the boss, the One who insists on overseeing every aspect of my life as a Christian. Christ exercises this not just in the power of His identity as Lord but also through the authority of what He has done.

> Do you not know that your body is a temple of the Holy Spirit who is in you, whom you have from God, and that you are not your own? For you have been bought with a price: there-fore glorify God in your body (1 Corinthians 6:19,20).

> ... knowing that you were not redeemed with perishable things like silver or gold from your futile way of life inherited from your fore-fathers, but with precious blood, as of a lamb unblemished and spotless, the blood of Christ (1 Peter 1:18,19).

> They sang a new song, saying, "Worthy art Thou to take the book, and to break its seals; for Thou wast slain, and didst purchase for God with Thy blood men from every tribe and tongue and people and nation" (Revelation 5:9).

Jesus, as Lord, absolutely owns every Christian; He bought them with the blood of the atonement shed at the cross. (See also Romans 14:7,8 and 2 Peter 2:1.) Jesus is Lord. He owns us. At any given time we are either in submission to that fact or in rebellion against it, but our stance changes nothing on Christ's side of things.

For those arguing that submission to anything destroys freedom, Jesus gives food for thought and reason to reconsider. Submission to a lord with absolute power enslaves and destroys freedom only if the lord is a tyrant. Submission to tyranny grinds the human spirit to fine powder. The yoke isn't the symbol that most people would choose for freedom. Animals in yoke and harness cannot go where they want but only where they're told.

I stood locked in the public stocks of the city of Colonial Williamsburg, Virginia. The wood chafed my neck and my wrists were clasped tight. The yoke, the stock, holds fast whatever or whoever gets locked up inside. But the yoke of lordship, of ownership, which Jesus places on all who are His is not the yoke of brute force but the yoke of grace.

> Come to Me, all who are weary and heavy-laden, and I will give you rest. Take My yoke upon you, and learn from Me, for I am gentle and humble in heart; and you shall find rest for your souls. For My yoke is easy, and My load is light (Matthew 11:28-30).

Agreeing with Christ

A second dimension of learning the texture of Christ's lordship grows out of submission—agreement. Agreement means we agree that Christ's will is right and good regardless of how severely His wishes fly in the face of our desires and opinions. One symptom of our self-centered times can be seen in our inflated view of our own opinion. We simply must get in our two cents' worth no matter what the subject.

In the process of having our say, we blur the line between having an opinion and knowing what we're talking about. I sat in the right-field stands at Tiger Stadium in Detroit one afternoon listening to all the "experts" telling the manager how to manage and the hitters how to hit. All opinions simply aren't of equal value.

A scan of the rebukes that Jesus gave the disciples shows that some of the sharpest ones came when disciples felt the need to question Jesus' actions or throw in their own opinions. Not only Christ's lordship but biblical teachings on judgment underscore the fact that in eternal spiritual matters of ultimate importance, our opinion will not be required. It will not even be asked. Yet today, in the face of the demise of societal belief in absolute truth, opinion is the new barometer of spiritual value and truth.

Being Christian, following Christ under submission to His lordship, includes agreeing that Jesus is the truth and that His Word is also truth. The agreement which this calls for is no sabotage of the mind. The command to love God with all our mind (Luke 10:27) flourishes under this willful submission; this is no intellectual suicide but stimulation. The history of Christianity resounds with the lives of men and women who, knowing Christ's yoke of lordship, rose to brilliance that otherwise would probably not have happened.

It lies woven into our spiritual genetic code, the image of God, to desire to know and find the true meaning of human existence. Agreeing wholeheartedly that Christ's will, not our own, is best is simply the truth. Our egos insist to be heard and to speak their piece. But if our opinions were genuinely as weighty and substantive as we like to think in our many vain moments, we would not have made the poor decisions, caused ourselves the heartbreaks, and suffered the spiritual aridity and barrenness that we have. The insistence to speak our disagreement, to be right, must die in order for joy in Christ to live.

Willing Obedience

A final and most important side to the texture of Christ's lordship is obedience. One of the recurring questions that resurfaces regularly among Christians involves discovering God's will. We act as if discerning His will is difficult: We use various formulas and approach the issue like a safecracker clicking tumblers into line to enter a vault. God does not reveal His will to satisfy our curiosity or so we can decide whether it compares favorably with the options we have already chosen to enshrine as treasures in our heart. God has no intention of revealing anything of His will to people He already knows are not predisposed to respond. Jesus is Lord. He commands; the servant obeys.

The one who does not obey Jesus Christ as Lord does not love Him because he idolatrously loves himself more. Jesus said quite plainly, "If you love Me, you will keep My commandments" (John 14:15). Only those obedient to Jesus' lordship will move to a deeper, more intimate relationship with Him.

> He who has My commandments and keeps them, he it is who loves Me; and he who loves Me shall be loved by My Father, and I will love him, and will disclose Myself to him (John 14:21).

> Jesus answered and said to him, "If anyone loves Me, he will keep My word; and My Father will love him, and We will come to him, and make Our abode with him" (John 14:23).

Keeping Christ's commandments, obeying His lordship, are not drudgery, punishment, or self-denigration under the heel of another person's ego.

> By this we know that we love the children of God, when we love God and observe His commandments. For this is the love of God, that we keep His commandments; and His commandments are not burdensome (1 John 5:2,3).

The servant who embraces the lordship of Jesus Christ will feel pangs, some stabbing deep, all through life over one issue or another to be brought under Christ's scrutiny and control. Instead of a once-for-all decision, we will come back again and again in repentance and tears.

But the one who kneels before Jesus as Lord knows two important truths. He knows that ultimately pleasing only himself is to feed not a legitimate hunger but rather the deepest lust of man that nothing can ever satisfy. He also knows that the holy will of a sovereign Lord alone is reality and the best that man can know, that to bow the knee and the heart to do Christ's will with all our might is to fulfill our destiny written in His heart before the ages. He can resonate with Paul:

> Whatever things were gain to me, those things I have counted as loss for the sake of Christ. More than that, I count all things to be loss in view of the surpassing value of knowing Christ Jesus my Lord, for whom I have suffered the loss of all things, and count them but rubbish in order that I may gain Christ (Philippians 3:7,8).

> Not one of us lives for himself, and not one dies for himself; for if we live, we live for the Lord, or if we die, we die for the Lord; therefore whether we live or die, we are the Lord's (Romans 14:7,8).

Learning the texture of the lordship of Jesus Christ readjusts the human heart until it pulsates most strongly only when it throbs in harmony with Christ's own heart. It is the primary spiritual discipline that we will spend our lives mastering. While it may never lose its bitter taste in given moments, the sweetness and rightness of each attempt, each victory, spurs us on to the next hurdle—which too will fall in Jesus' name as we strive obediently toward it.

Embracing God

God's Splints on Weak Spirits

Spiritual disciplines evoke interesting responses in the minds of Christians. One line of thought says that disciplines are for eccentric, bizarre, or exceptional Christians. Monks and mystics who didn't have to buck freeway traffic, run the kids' carpool, or negotiate the aisles in the supermarket had time and the inclination for that stuff, but not us. Wearing hair shirts or sackcloth, sleeping on stone floors, taking icy baths at unusual hours, going without food, and praying for hours at a time all appear about as attractive as a root canal job.

Then there are the spiritual athletes. They salivate at the mention of spiritual disciplines. Where some couldn't care less, these can't get enough. Their quiet times resemble an Olympic workout. I remember well when my own devotional life had to include an introductory reading from a devotional guide plus a daily Bible reading of eight chapters a day in an elaborate system taking me through the Old Testament twice and the New Testament once in a year. I also did work on Scripture memory and prayed both through a detailed prayer manual and a guide for interceding for the nations of the world. I concluded with worship and praise sung from a hymnal. All this was supposed to fit into one hour!

What place does spiritual discipline have in a life? Some disciplines function as spiritual life support—equivalents of eating, breathing, and exercise. Bible study, prayer, giving, ministry, and the like sustain us all our Christian lives, maintaining basic spiritual health. While these should be tailored to individual need, they are essential and we neglect them at our peril.

But we ignore another subtler class of disciplines. One day at work we put in a new sidewalk. We cut and laid two-by-fours as forms and then poured the concrete. The sidewalk would never have taken shape if not for the forms. God imposes short-term or long-term disciplines on our behavior and thoughts as the forms of real observable righteousness that Jesus Christ wants to infuse into our lives. A discipline is like a splint on a weak joint or limb that remains until the strength is back.

Disciplines for Growth

As a new Christian in the Jesus movement, I began my Christian life with many others who came out of the robustly sinful ethos of the counterculture of the late sixties. It wasn't at all uncommon to hear that some who had been particularly sexually active were fasting relationally. Some men could only see women as sexual objects. Some women gave their bodies away indiscriminately to feel loved or in attempts to fill other deep voids and insecurities in their lives.

Without any human prompting, God's Spirit seemed to say, "You can't handle sexuality right now. Until you can see the opposite sex as brothers or sisters in Christ instead of a body to be used solely for fleeting pleasure or a temporary compensation for deep needs and hurts within, no dating. You're to have no social contact except in groups of Christians. And no touching—not even a finger!"

This sounds ridiculous to many people, but not to those serious enough about becoming like Christ to grapple fiercely with sexual sin deeply ingrained. Looking at AIDS, the incredible spread of other sexually transmitted diseases (a number of them incurable), the continuing high number of pregnancies out of wedlock, and the surprisingly high rate of Christian young people sexually active, we can hardly say that there is no need for such measures.

But disciplines from God in our Christian growth come in more subtle forms. One person I know is bound by the Lord to pray daily for those against whom he has a bad attitude for any reason. He asks God to give them everything he would request for himself. We tend to freeze people in their deficiencies, particularly when their deficiencies have wounded or hurt us.

Doing this takes a big first step toward creating fertile ground for grudges, resentment, and hatred to root. Instead of brooding over slights and hurts of all sizes against him, my friend sees how empty he is of Christ's love toward others. After all, even pagans can love people who have never laid a glove on them (Matthew 5:43-47).

He also sees the people as Christ does. This enables him to drop petty aggravations before they soar into something worse. Because of this, he can actively serve in their lives without regard for their regard of him. Faces from past and present come and go on his mental list, but the discipline to pray remains. Some on the list have become friends; some remain unreachable in his past. But his obedience to the forms of loving others as Christ did releases the Spirit to continue pouring out and shaping up the reality of it in his life.

Spiritual Anorexia?

One thing spiritual disciplines do not do is to serve as ends in themselves toward pleasing God. People who fast are not better Christians than people who do not. In the last few years, we have learned much about eating disorders such as anorexia nervosa. The anorexic obsesses over weight loss to the degree that he or she will starve himself and resort to injurious doses of laxatives.

Newer discoveries show that some anorexics resort to compulsive exercise: What at first looks helpful and healthy is actually harmful. Marathon spiritual performances don't impress God. They may be nothing more than spiritual anorexia. The Pharisees gave, fasted, and prayed, but to no avail. My devotional pattern described earlier was more aimed at getting everything into my hour rather than with actually meeting God. I was meeting my own standards of perfection instead of drinking deeply of His grace. I was exercising but starving.

Olympic medalists don't get up at four in the morning and run hundreds of unseen miles to impress others. They do whatever they do in training because something they cherish and long for has reached out from the other side of effort and exertion to seize them deep within with a promise of hope.

So it is with spiritual disciplines: They are the lifeline to vital life in Christ as well as forms for the infusion of visible righteousness we have thirsted for. We submit and perform not because the disciplines are easy, fun, or desirable in themselves. We submit in the promise of hope in Christ—hope in knowing Him and becoming like Him. In these, as with lesser hopes, Jesus Christ will never disappoint.

14

The Essence of Growth

I f one word could summarize spiritual growth, that word would be "changed." When Jesus Christ entered our lives, He may have loved us as we were, but He has no intention of leaving us that way.

> Our citizenship is in heaven, from which also we eagerly wait for a Savior, the Lord Jesus Christ; who will transform the body of our humble state into conformity with the body of His glory, by the exertion of the power that He has even to subject all things to Himself (Philippians 3:20,21).

> We all, with unveiled face beholding as in a mirror the glory of the Lord, are being transformed into the same image from glory to glory, just as from the Lord, the Spirit (2 Corinthians 3:18).

Embracing God

The price of spiritual growth always comes down to change. God's Spirit shows us something new of Christ, something never dreamed of or something resisted as false, and we balk. But we must not. To refuse to be changed by God's Spirit under Christ's hand is to stiffen and ossify. Change doesn't always approach like a friend. More often than not change comes as an intrusion, sometimes an invasion.

The Pains of Change

In my teens, change was no problem; I bounced off it without realizing it. Now I notice it with more than a passing agitation for at least three reasons. First, change is no problem for me as long as it leaves untouched the things I care about. Phone mail can be a nuisance but it's not worth an ulcer, so we coexist. But some things change that disturb me deeply. It bothers me that my children do not and have not had the degree of freedom I had at their age. It's not just my imagination romanticizing the past; danger very present now makes some freedoms I enjoyed unthinkable for them. They don't miss what they never knew, but I feel the loss for them. Something has changed that I care about, but I'm powerless to recapture it.

Another reason I often fail to see change as a friend is that it doesn't usually knock; it almost always enters my life uninvited. I grew a beard this summer for the first time; I'm not sure why. Some say it will give me an attitude. (I think it provides a good excuse for the attitude I already have!) People joke around about my "salt-and-pepper" beard. I'm still looking for the "pepper"; the "salt" is sure plain enough without my having requested it.

Gravity sneaked up on me without my permission, and I don't remember coveting the pain in my lower back when I get out of bed. Neither do I remember being asked when values such as marital fidelity, conceiving children out of love and actually giving them birth, and not zoning God out of all sections of public life fell cheapened into the dirt and were trampled underfoot.

Finally, change comes often more swiftly than I can adjust to it. I can perform about one-third of the functions on a standard pocket calculator. I still scratch out my writing with pen and paper instead of using a word processor. I finally learned how to actually time and tape something on the VCR. But I stand gibbering like a technological zombie as I look at the remote control for my son's stack stereo, the one that appears to have enough functions to control 60 percent of all satellite hardware currently in orbit!

Change flies past us incredibly rapidly today, and not just in terms of science and technology. Morals (public and private), sociological models of the family, and the world-view undergirding our lives have all gone through much more change in the last 30 years than anyone could have imagined. The more intent we become on clinging to the familiar, the more the familiar is torn from our grasp. The rapidity of change doesn't even leave time for us to assess the new, let alone adjust to it.

Flexing for Growth

Not only is change often unwelcome in our lives, but our ability to flex to it decreases with age. Yet change is the essence of growth in Christ. The Holy Spirit always works toward the uprooting of wrong actions and attitudes, replacing them with His fruit (Galatians 5:22,23). There can be no greater degree of change than our being conformed to the image of Jesus Christ. Sometimes our resistance to change has blacker roots than just our irritation with the change process. John wrote, "Light is come into the world, and men loved the darkness rather than the light, for their deeds were evil" (John 3:19). Spiritual growth sometimes means that the Holy Spirit will raise issues we would rather not deal with.

Perhaps we foolishly thought we could hide the sin, if not from God, at least from others. Maybe we lie to ourselves that the sin isn't all that bad or even there at all. Whether we care to face what is on the Holy Spirit's agenda or not isn't an issue. Much of our growling and grumbling against change in things pertaining to the kingdom of God is nothing more than veiled resentment of conviction of sin. People under conviction of sin are often angry and looking for targets.

Sometimes we grumble against change because we don't see God's hand in the new. No Christian, including the disciples, ever saw completely what God was doing through Jesus Christ. Our prejudices, our immersion in tradition, and our spiritual dullness may have us digging in our heels against the change that God desires to bring about in our lives.

Whether it is the actual difficulty of coping with change, or being unwilling to face the need for change where God has pinpointed it, or just spiritual nearsightedness, we are not left to ourselves: The Holy Spirit stands as not only the converter but the helper. Transitions seemingly impossible to face may loom up unexpectedly or approach with a steady pace we cannot outrun.

The change that Saul of Tarsus went through at conversion was staggering: from persecutor of the faith to its champion. The shattering that came at his conversion, followed by the subsequent reconstruction of all his life and thought, must have been far more traumatic than we commonly suppose.

Paying the Price

We catch just a glimpse of the trauma by looking at the struggles of one of our contemporaries. Francis Schaeffer left a church in St. Louis to minister to young wayward skeptics, burnouts from the drug culture, and anyone suffering from spiritual disillusionment at what would come to be known as L'Abri in Switzerland. Schaeffer knew that dealing with the lives and spiritual choices of broken people would be more demanding than anything he had ever faced. He paced the attic floor of their home rethinking every tenet of the Christian faith, pushing each one to see if there was a breaking point. At times his wife, Edith, feared for his sanity. But the vigorous intellectual rigor that emerged from such change impacted a generation. The grappling with change could not have been less with Paul.

The Holy Spirit is our helper amidst change sent from God's hand. His presence is like oil poured out to reduce friction and wear. The greater and more pressing the change, the more He is poured out. Change is the design of spiritual growth. It may hurt to leave behind some cherished memories, forms, and artifacts of faith that are now obsolete. It may hurt to have our fingers pried from things that have come to mean too much, or to be made to face and repent of sin. The Holy Spirit of God anoints us against the heat of friction that would otherwise threaten to tear us down or shake us apart.

Everything changes—both the trivial and the important. It comes without invitation and faster than we can cope with when we sense its onset. Even heaven and earth as they now stand will change (Matthew 24:35; 2 Peter 3:7,10).

The change that crashes into our lives sometimes feels like our heaven and earth are sliding away. Can we root our lives, the fabric of our being, in anything that will hold secure? Just as He was before time existed and will be after time is swallowed up, "Jesus Christ is the same yesterday and today, yes and forever" (Hebrews 13:8). No matter how unexpected or deep the change that comes (and ultimately all of it comes from God's sovereign hand), Jesus Christ stands spanning space and time as our only security. When spiritual growth means change, we can cling tight with no fear of turning those rough corners.

Dark Nights and Dry Times

The high plains of the Texas Panhandle spawn a hearty, tough people. The land demands it. Grassland and semi-arid desert, it stretches vast and wide-looking, as if you could see from Mexico to Canada by a turn of the head.

They harness the wind in west Texas, but nobody can slow it down. The trees grow gnarled and tough, all bent to the same angles from hot wind that blows without letup. It parches rivers down to dry silt beds sprouting weeds, and over the centuries it has eroded high mesas down to low ones.

The life of every Christian peaks and drops. We may have experiences of rich intimacy and depth. We will also feel our feet on the crumbling edge of despair and doubt. But we will spend most of our Christian experience somewhere in between, crossing flat country where there's little shade and the hot wind never stops blowing. Fatigue and dryness creep on slowly but surely, sinking deep into our bones and spirit. God's voice and hand may seem far away, more a memory of earlier times when our walk with God held the spring of youth, a vestige of days we despair of retrieving.

But what we have come to know as wilderness experiences do not necessarily come to us this way. Scripture shows that these are neither to be sought in monastic quest to please God nor merely to be endured.

Wilderness experiences are carefully timed by God. Jesus was specifically led, even driven, into the wilderness by the Holy Spirit (Mark 1:12; also Matthew 4:1; Luke 4:1). While some of our dryness stems from the deadness of active sin, that doesn't account for all of it. God Himself will steer us onto dry high plains and into deep waterless arroyos, for apart from them certain deep things that only His love can do will never happen. This is important to know, since attitude is everything in a spiritual wilderness.

Two men suffered heart attacks followed by bypass surgeries. One spent his convalescence reading new things that stretched his mind, in good conversations with his wife and children, investing wisely in what mattered. The other man lounged listlessly on the couch, watching soap operas for four months and slipping into depression. Dry flat times in spirit are no time to walk dull and thickly through our days. Our lives move under the orchestrating touch of the Holy Spirit's hand, whose dynamics we do not always understand.

We should stop lusting after escape or poutingly demanding explanations like a whiny and petulant child. As long as we haven't engineered our own shipwreck, our wildernesses are as much under the Holy Spirit's imprimatur as was Jesus'. It is a time to listen sharply for the voice of God—easily drowned in the roar of the rush of the city or daily life, but which soars high on the hot winds of wilderness. It is not a time to rebel against what we know to be true by embracing the lie of what our emotions and circumstances tell us.

Jesus was filled with the Holy Spirit just before that same Spirit compelled Him to enter the wilderness where He fasted and prayed for 40 days. To merely stand in the wilderness requires all the power and sustaining grace that God can pour out. Those standing in a wilderness can look to Jesus Christ and know that all the power and grace the Spirit can pour out stands poised over them every minute. Wildernesses can seem barren and unending, but they are never accidents. God may be blending at least three things into our lives in wilderness times that don't often come in other ways.

Wildernesses clean us out. I used to unload trucks at a hospital in the Chicago area. Once every summer I would unload four large barrels of acid. That was when the maintenance crew shut down and drained the huge boilers in the hospital basement so the accumulated mineral deposits built up over a year of heavy use could be cleaned out. Strong acid was the only thing that could do it.

Wildernesses shut down all normal operations of the life and spirit so deep cleansing can take place. The apostle Paul knew his wildernesses, particularly at the beginning of his Christian life. Struck blind in his encounter with Christ, Paul was led helpless into Damascus, where he sat for three days without sight and without food and water—

and Paul didn't know at the time that it would be just three days.

Did he sit chewing on a deep mortification at how blind and cruel he had been and that the only thing his religious zeal had accomplished was to make him a virulent enemy of God? Probably, since repentance has that kind of flavor to it. (Sin not worth some honest grieving has not been seen rightly, and now Paul was seeing it.) During those three days, while the miracle of grace soaked in, Paul's enmity against God's people drained from his heart like the sludge dripping from an old crankcase. Unless old angers, hatred, and bitterness drain, new grace may not penetrate very deep.

Busyness keeps us preoccupied and locked up in the denial caused by frantic routine. Wilderness, even the wilderness of three days of helpless darkness, slams all of that to a halt. God has His darkrooms today as well, where He shuts us down so old debris can be wheelbarrowed out—cardiac care units, maximum-security mental-health lock-ups, prison cells, or a lonely apartment where nobody comes to call. While at first these may appear to be nothing more than varieties of hell, these and other experiences have been the wildernesses that have birthed lives rich and powerful for God and His kingdom. The life that emerges transcends the darkness endured, whether it was three days or seemingly three eternities.

A New Perspective

A second cutting edge of wilderness times lies in the new perspective gained. Not only individuals but nations enter wildernesses. Israel's liberation from Egypt through Moses surely revealed God's sheer power. But the mass of people who stood on dry land beside the Red Sea watching the bodies of Pharaoh's crack troops wash ashore were far from being the nation of Israel that God ultimately intended. The wilderness of Sinai would be the classroom where they would learn.

There the children of Israel learned of God's ability to provide physical needs. They saw His majesty and holiness both in the blazing of Mount Sinai and the law engraved on stone tablets brought down by Moses. They saw His wisdom and guidance in the pillar of fire at night and cloud by day, as well as in the smaller detailed temporary restrictions given through Moses in regulating infectious disease, settling civil disputes, etc. They learned what it meant to worship God through the construction, design, and use of the tabernacle.

God reinforced what they had already seen of His protection through miraculous intervention against their enemies. The wilderness of Sinai was to be a school where a multitude would be molded into a new identity, would see themselves in a new light and a much different perspective than the slaves they used to be. The school became a grave only for those (sadly, a whole generation) who could never be rid either of their taste for Egypt or their desire to be satisfied by anything outside themselves.

But those who followed the priests carrying the ark of the covenant across the Jordan River were different people; they walked again on dry land amidst risen water, but with shoulders squared by faith that would conquer the land God had promised—and this time with no looking back.

Paul, too, may have known this. In Galatians 1:17 he refers cryptically to time spent in Arabia sometime between his earliest Christian days in Damascus and his first visit to Jerusalem as a believer. The time may have been as long as a year, depending on how the chronology of Paul's life is constructed.

What was he doing? Paul never divulges how that time was spent. Some say in ministry. But Paul had a brilliant mind steeped in the Scriptures and honed sharp as a razor's edge under the tutelage of the great rabbinic scholar Gamaliel. With the great ministry that lay in store for Paul (although unknown to him then), could not the Spirit of God have led Paul away to recalibrate all of this biblical knowledge and insight, refocusing it with Jesus Christ as the center? Could Paul have spent time rethinking every point of his theology, retooling it and discovering in awe how the Hebrew Scriptures radiate with Christ's promise and presence, taking every thought captive (2 Corinthians 10:5) for his newfound Savior and bathing the quest in worship and prayer?

Valuable jewels are never displayed after the cutting but only after the polishing. Out of Damascus, Paul was eager but raw-cut. Whatever happened in Arabia, the apostle emerged as a chisel that would crack an empire with new vision, toughness, and strength.

The Fiery Love of God

A final part of wilderness experience, and possibly the part which marks the human spirit more deeply than the other two, is being shut away from all else to the fiery jealous love of God. All human understanding, concern, and support are stripped away until all that is left is God Himself.

This explains John the Baptist. At a young age he left his parents and lived many years out in the wild (Luke 1:80). Years of solitude with God honed John's life until it burned with the clean economy of a single white-hot flame. Intensity and passion come not with emotion and froth but rise blazing out of depth and solitude with God. When John finally appeared to stand as the forerunner to the Messiah, his life cut deep swaths of righteousness among the people of his day.

While Jesus needs no forerunners today, where are those whose lives have been threaded in the wilderness into wicks where the flame of God's love can burn? The church needs them more than it can know. These are not tame people, but neither are the times we live in.

The God who closes us up to Himself in a wilderness experience is jealous. He waxes passionately toward those He loves, and He will not be ignored. Jacob's time of severe wilderness lasted one night (Genesis 32:24-32). Having left his conniving uncle Laban, Jacob and his family now stood confronted by Esau, the brother cheated years earlier of his birthright, and 400 men. Sending livestock and family on ahead, Jacob lingered behind alone when suddenly he found himself wrestling for his life against a stranger.

During the struggle Jacob realized that his opponent was more than human. Collapsing to the ground with a dislocated hip, Jacob pleaded for His blessing. God had loved Jacob and revealed Himself to this wayward conniver for years, but the only thing Jacob had ever trusted was his own wits. Now alone by the riverbank, Jacob utters in pain the words God longed to hear: "I will not let you go unless you bless me" (Genesis 32:26).

If we run from God's love long enough, He can be provoked to a jealousy for our hearts which boxes us off in some wilderness where He will pin us to the ground to love us. If our stubbornness persists, we run the risk of encountering the fierceness of His love—fierce enough to leave a limp in our spirit as a reminder that the love of a jealous God is nothing to spurn lightly. Grace pushed away can push back harder than we think.

Hiking in the Canyon

My kids and I hiked in the Grand Canyon; hiking into the canyon is much easier than hiking out. Slogging up steep trails in heat approaching 90 degrees, we plodded along thinking we would never get back to the trailhead. We heard footsteps crunching briskly along behind us, and soon a voice chirped in an unmistakable Australian accent, "G'day, mate! Great day for this. Keep at it. See you at the top!" A wiry little man carrying a full backpack stepped smartly past us with as much trouble as a Grand Prix race car would have passing a tricycle. We were too busy gasping for air to speak, but we looked at each other as he disappeared around the trail.

At a rest shelter further up, we caught up to this man and sat in the shade listening to his stories. He had traversed the Grand Canyon three or four times, most of the world's major deserts, and hundreds of miles of Australian outback. Something about that kind of barren wilderness kept calling him. His intimacy with land that showed no mercy to intruders had leathered his skin while tightening and toughening his body. From terrain that could kill those not respecting it, he had mined jewels that shone in his eyes as he spoke of sunsets on the Gobi Desert and feeling the night wind of the outback.

So it is with all whom God calls to a wilderness. Precious dimensions of life in Christ, real jewels, are there to be found. We are not to shrink from, and therefore squander, wildernesses brought at God's hand, but are to mine them instead. Those who do so under the Spirit's leading will find Christlike riches unknown to those choosing the paths that are always level and where the grass is always lush and green.

Spiritual growth eventually carries a tearstained price tag redeemable only in a wilderness of God's design. It is no coincidence that the church is growing most rapidly today not in the industrialized West but in Third World nations— Central and South America, sub-Saharan Africa, and much of Asia. The church behind the collapsed "Iron Curtain" is numerically beginning to increase rapidly.

How is all this happening without North American church growth experts and the clout of Western wealth and technology? A Korean pastor of one of the world's largest churches was asked why the churches of Korea were growing not only in numbers but in depth. His answer speaks for the Third World church. He pondered for a long moment and said:

> I think it is because we lived under severe
> Japanese persecution for so long. We learned
> to have no hope in ourselves, but only in God.

Embracing God

And we learned to pray. We have been a suffering church and, therefore, a praying church. That is what I think explains it.[19]

What a catalyst for church growth! Scripture says that God is the "God of all comfort" (2 Corinthians 1:3). But God will lavish no comfort on us that leaves us soft, self-indulgent, and whining for more of what we have already grown fat on. To grow is to stretch, and to stretch is sometimes to hurt in body, mind, or spirit.

To refuse to grow is to begin to die. No honest Christian can live with that choice for long; we have simply seen and tasted too much. The stretch to embrace God is worth it not because of the benefits to us but because of the God we embrace.

15

⚜

Every Life a Masterpiece

Michelangelo, the famous artist and sculptor, supposedly once bought a large chunk of marble. He and others strained and sweated to move the stone to his studio. Someone remarked that this seemed to be a lot of trouble and asked the great artist why he bothered. Michelangelo replied, "Because there is an angel trapped in there crying to be let out."

Jesus Christ does not save people from sin just to transport them to heaven upon their death. He saves us because something deep within us, the image of God in us, cries to be let out, to be released, to be restored. Biblical salvation begins with accepting Jesus Christ but continues on in a process, complete only in heaven but observable now, where we become what only God can make us.

Human Need and Longing

Our inner landscape rolls, rises, and falls according to

some well-defined needs. The needs of our heart may take on the shape of our culture but do not originate there. They rise as longings of the human heart that outline the shape of our creation—the image of God in us. While we can know partial satisfaction of these longings now, lasting fulfillment seems to evaporate and elude us. But we can never rest or know much peace in our lives while these longings lie unmet.

First among these is the need to be loved. We live in a love-starved society. Everybody wants it but fewer and fewer seem to be able to find it. Too many people carry a vacuum in their adult lives from parents and others who failed them relationally. This vacuum fills up with anger and sometimes leads to depression. People who received inadequate love growing up often make poor relationship choices in marriage. Sometimes we're just nearsighted and selfish. We look at love as primarily a feeling or something to get rather than to give, and our love relationships implode. Epidemic loneliness eats away silently at millions of people.

Love is simply the greatest thing which the heart of God offers to the heart of man. Love isn't something God has, love is what God *is* (1 John 4:8,16). The love that God gives offers two magnificent qualities to wayward, groping humanity. One is its commitment. God's love toward us is a rock-ribbed commitment that He makes to us even though He knows more about us than we will admit to ourselves. Nothing we can pull out of a closet or our subconscious can shock Him into not loving us. That is why Paul could write so grandly:

> I am convinced that neither death, nor life, nor angels, nor principalities, nor things present, nor things to come, nor powers, nor height, nor depth, nor any other created thing, shall be able to separate us from the love of God, which is in Christ Jesus our Lord (Romans 8:38,39).

Undeserved Love

A second trait flows from the first. Because God's love is one that cannot be destroyed by the unknown (since He sees all things at all times), His love is undeserved. Who can rightfully lay claim to a love like that? God's love is mercy where only judgment is required. The nation of Israel, after 60 years of captivity, had returned to the land and started to rebuild. The first reconstruction would be the temple (Ezra 3:1-13). The day the foundation was completed, the nation gathered for worship and praise. The people cried out with a great shout while the trumpets sounded.

The cries, however, had a strange mix. Many of the priests and elders who had lived all through the 60 years of captivity could remember the earlier temple—Solomon's temple. They could also remember the apostasy and idolatry that drove the nation of Israel into judgment. Many of them had probably despaired of ever coming back to their homeland again. But now not only were they back, but the temple was going back up. The old-timers wept while younger men laughed and cheered. After all the terrible sin of the nation, God had been so kind. No one understood it better on that day than the graybeards.

It takes the seasoning of years to appreciate grace. We sat one night at a concert with over ten thousand young people. The singer had been good, challenging the people to aggressive Christian discipleship. Two rows in front of me, a young man sporting a Christian T-shirt leaped to his feet repeatedly, thrusting his hand into the air in a "one way" sign. I grinned, appreciating his zeal. I also wondered how much he understood of what it would really cost to "lay his life down for Christ and take this city for Jesus."

I saw myself 24 years earlier and remembered both the commitments I had made to God and how I have repeatedly aborted them, only to come back to His love, which I always found waiting. I had always believed in grace, God's undeserved love. Now, though, I am one of the graybeards who sometimes remember more of failure than of victory, and grace now towers over what I knew in younger years. God has had a lot to forgive over the years. The amazing thing is that He did.

The human heart cries out for love. God cries out with more love than the human heart can hold—any heart, no matter what is inside. As precious as human love in relationships can be, death ensures that even the strongest relationships on earth will end. Our hunger for love was never meant to find permanent fulfillment through earthly avenues.

Longing to Be Known

We also long to be understood, to be known. One of life's genuinely satisfying experiences is to be truly understood. One of the frustrations of joys and agonies of pain is being locked up alone with our feelings, having no one who truly knows us or how we feel.

I did a stint as a hospital chaplain as a very young Christian. Visiting different patients, I did something very foolish. I reassured patient after patient that I knew exactly how they felt. Walking into one room, I met a middle-aged woman and asked her why she was in the hospital. She replied, "I'm here for a complete hysterectomy and I expect to be a new woman." My mind started to kick in with my pat answers but nothing came out of my mouth. I had nothing to say. We can brutalize others by callously assuming we know what's going on inside when it's highly likely we do not.

God knows us like no other person. Who knows the creation better than the designer?

> He Himself knows our frame; He is mindful that we are but dust (Psalm 103:14).

He knows our real potentials; He instilled them in us. God also understands our weakness and limitations—our strength of body and mind, our capacities to absorb pain and experience joy. How we long to have someone know us like this! But maybe we haven't had someone who could be trusted, or maybe we just didn't know how to open up. Whether we have or not, our disappointments and intimacies stand as yearnings for or partial fulfillments of something that only God can fully give.

> Now we see in a mirror dimly, but then face
> to face; now I know in part, but then I shall
> know fully just as I also have been fully known
> (1 Corinthians 13:12).

We also have lives with meaning. A psychological study team paid people to hit a piece of wood with the blunt edge of an ax. The money was good, but even those who gladly started quit before very long. "It's no use," one said; "I just need to see the chips fly." We all need to see the chips fly, need to know that our life makes a mark. Our frustration comes in looking for meaning that lasts inside ourselves. Our lives were meant to throb with the purposes of the God who made us. Lives that Jesus touched instantly took on new significance as He became the center. A few lives touch the ages, but any life touching Jesus Christ makes chips fly beyond time.

The Frame of Our Lives

We long to have integrated lives. Yet most of the time we treat our lives as if they consisted of various compartments or segments. Some compartments do well while others seem to stand in constant disrepair. Some lives unravel all around the edge. A woman sat on her front porch doing needlepoint when her pastor drove up. As they talked, she said, "My life is like this needlework. I need a frame to keep it from unraveling." We all need a frame, something that will integrate our lives. How difficult to find within ourselves something that will lastingly do it!

The needs and longings to be loved, to be known, to have meaning and for integration in our lives owe their presence in our lives to God; He placed them there. As He works toward satisfying those longings, God never works capriciously but always toward a definite end.

> I am confident of this very thing, that He who began a good work in you will perfect it until the day of Christ Jesus (Philippians 1:6).

> We are His workmanship, created in Christ Jesus for good works, which God prepared beforehand, that we should walk in them (Ephesians 2:10).

Like Michelangelo, God knows exactly what is trapped inside us and knows how to release it. The cross evidences how serious He is about completing His redemption in our lives and about fulfilling the yearnings which nothing on this planet can completely satisfy.

A Solid Hope

Disillusionment in life's deepest concerns runs deep in a life where hope lies shattered. A man bitter against all religious groups told me of a group he fell into years before. The leader told him to climb the mountain outside of town, whereupon the young disciple would hear the voice of God. The young man did what he was told. "You know what God said to me up there? He said, 'Phil, you're a fool!'" Angry and feeling used, the now-older man stood bitter and hard.

Scripture writes of hope in Jesus Christ as a hope that did not disappoint (Romans 5:5; Hebrews 6:18,19). Other spiritual options do. The Hindu belief in cycles of karma expressed through reincarnation holds no certain hope. The hypercommitment and devotion of many cultists flames out over time, and then they find it difficult to extract themselves from the group. Evangelical churches and Christians may also disappoint, but never Jesus Christ. Hope in Him has a substance now that will never fade as time goes on. Jesus brings the gospel of change into our lives—change that lasts, concrete steps from death to life.

Hope in Jesus Christ, in God's determination to produce Christ's image in us, brings visible healing to body and mind. Dramatics and theater cheapen healing, casting it in poor repute. But Jesus, in the Gospels, made a great difference in people's lives. In body and mind, Jesus touched lives then and still does today. Thousands of people in churches today know something of this even if their church either does not believe in or does not actively practice any kind of healing ministry.

While God does this (sometimes unbidden), healing is not an end in itself but an extension of His grace. Quality of life as God sees it emanates from a healthy spirit. The tangible foretastes of all that God will ultimately do to redeem His image in us deal ultimately with the heart. Scripture says, "Watch over your heart with all diligence, for from it flow the springs of life" (Proverbs 4:23). Jesus stressed, "The mouth speaks out of that which fills the heart" (Matthew 12:34; see also Matthew 15:18; Luke 6:45).

That's why Jesus often forgave sins in connection with His healings. Sometimes the body is sick because the heart needs attention; Jesus never deals with the weed without removing the root. To seize quality of life the world deals with externals, hoping that wholeness will sink in. As we embrace God, His Spirit begins in the heart and works out. Michelangelo may have had no choice but to work from the outside in, but God begins in the heart. Christ promises no quality of life that starts anywhere else.

The Completed Work of God

Jesus Christ can provide partial satisfactions of our deepest longings here on earth, but we should remember some important disclaimers. First, God's job is not primarily to protect us. He is not bound to shield us from the

fragility of our human condition. At times He will allow us
to feel it deeply so we will lean on Him, trusting Him all the
more. There is no healing of body or mind that will forestall
death. Both Lazarus and the daughter of Jairus, whom
Jesus raised from the dead, still subsequently died.

God's fulfillments of our deepest yearning is never
promised on our terms or along our lines of expectation.
We are never promised immunity from aging, sickness,
pain, and death. While Christ will banish these someday
and deals with them to a degree now, His goal is to transform us, and not just to eradicate the things dragging us
down in this life.

Many Christians become absorbed with what God can
do now; to them heaven is just going to happen later. The
truth is that our bodies, our lives, and even this planet
simply cannot bear the full weight of God's completed
work. Everything we know of human history and everything making up mankind's earthly future stand as God's
workbench. We have heard the stories of people building
boats in their basement and then not being able to get them
out the door. God's deepest works are never designed to
make us content with what we are or with what He can
make of us now. God creates longings and has designs that
the workshop cannot hold; these can only know fulfillment
in eternity. The apostle Paul relished this, the Christian's
hope.

> I consider that the sufferings of this present
> time are not worthy to be compared with the
> glory that is to be revealed to us. For the anx-
> ious longing of the creation waits eagerly for
> the revealing of the sons of God. For the cre-
> ation was subjected to futility, not of its own
> will, but because of Him who subjected it, in
> hope that the creation itself also will be set free
> from its slavery to corruption into the freedom
> of the glory of the children of God. For we

know that the whole creation groans and suffers the pains of childbirth together until now. And not only this, but also we ourselves, having the first fruits of the Spirit, even we ourselves groan within ourselves, waiting eagerly for our adoption as sons, the redemption of our body (Romans 8:18-23).

We know that if the earthly tent which is our house is torn down, we have a building from God, a house not made with hands, eternal in the heavens. For indeed in this house we groan, longing to be clothed with our dwelling from heaven; inasmuch as we, having put it on, shall not be found naked. For indeed while we are in this tent, we groan, being burdened, because we do not want to be unclothed, but to be clothed, in order that what is mortal may be swallowed up by life. Now He who prepared us for this very purpose is God, who gave to us the Spirit as a pledge (2 Corinthians 5:1-5).

Our citizenship is in heaven, from which also we eagerly wait for a Savior, the Lord Jesus Christ; who will transform the body of our humble state into conformity with the body of His glory, by the exertion of the power that He has even to subject all things to Himself (Philippians 3:20,21).

The writer of Hebrews frames well how this hope rests on the Christian life the longer we go on.

All these died in faith, without receiving the promises, but having seen them and having welcomed them from a distance, and having confessed that they were strangers and exiles on the earth. For those who say such things

make it clear that they are seeking a country of
their own. And indeed if they had been thinking of that country from which they went out,
they would have had opportunity to return.
But as it is, they desire a better country, that is a
heavenly one. Therefore God is not ashamed
to be called their God; for He has prepared a
city for them (Hebrews 11:13-16).

The older I get the more often I feel like a peg more
square in a hole more round. One sign of spiritual growth
is a heartache, the feeling of not belonging or fitting in—
sometimes even feeling like an alien or stranger among the
people of God for whom the baubles of the world outshine
the riches of Christ. Jesus Christ has no desire to reinforce
our attachments here. Embracing God in the face of Jesus
Christ weans us from the holds that the world lays so
deeply on us.

Running the Last Steps

Heaven is far more than the absence of sickness, pain,
and death. Scripture says that God will wipe away all tears
(Revelation 7:17; 21:4). But if there are no tears, there must
be new ways to express joy that we don't know about now.
The pure, undiluted wholeness only Christ can bring about
will shine radiantly through us brighter than the noonday
sun. As surely as Michelangelo freed his angel from the
stone, Christ will have cut us free from every encumbrance
prone to body and mind. Samuel Shoemaker wrote tell-
ingly of this just before he died.

As I sit in the study on a beautiful, cool Au-
gust afternoon, I look back with many thanks.
It has been a great run. I wouldn't have missed
it for anything. Much could and should have
been better, and I have by no means done what
I should have done with all that I have been

given. But the over-all experience of being alive has been a thrilling experience. I believe that death is a doorway to more of it: clearer, cleaner, better, with more of the secret opened than locked. . . . I believe that I shall see Him and know Him, and that eternity will be an endless opportunity to consort with the great souls and the lesser ones who have entered into the freedom of the heavenly city. It is His forgiveness and grace that give confidence and not merits of our own.[20]

One can't miss the quiet yet eager anticipation in Shoemaker's voice. He walks the last steps with a sure, firm stride. I plan to run. Nothing will ever eclipse the embrace of God in the face of Jesus in the lives of those who know it. Heaven stores up precious reunions as well as new meetings with lives touched by Christ across the centuries.

Heaven's beauty will enhance the awe of its Creator. We will not walk around like a bunch of camera-toting tourists, because we won't be tourists at all. Christ's glory will fit us as a tailored glove; we will be home in the truest sense ever known. And we will rush to the feet of Christ, content to lie there for the first thousand years of eternity.

But for now this certain hope draws all of us who embrace God, for the time draws near when the embracing will be in person and will never reach an end.

EPILOGUE

Plunge In!

Nature spawns some of its rivers in high country. And where flowing springwater and snow runoff meet sharp drops in elevation, God gives adventure and beauty wrapped in a single gift: whitewater.

In the last few years we have latched on to this passion with every ride, leaving us hungry for a bigger one next time. After one particular shot down a stretch of the Arkansas River in Colorado, our guide talked about a swim she took the day before.

She had paddled in a raft with six novices. After a couple of miles of easy water where they learned to maneuver, they heard the roar of the first major rapids around the bend. As they came within a few yards of the rapids, a large hole, gaping wide and foaming deep, yawned open directly in their path.

At that moment a 250-pound football player sitting toward the rear completely panicked and jumped to his feet (the whitewater equivalent of dancing on the wing of a jetliner in flight). With terror in his eyes he spun around and grabbed the guide in a bear hug. Both of them flipped over the back of the raft into the water and five novices plunged into class IV whitewater knowing that the only one who knew how to steer just fell out.

Why do I love whitewater? Canoers, kayakers, and rafters can't always put it into words but know it instinctively: The thrill of the ride stands out. There is something intimate about interacting with nature in power that breeds awe and reverence. This deepens as the paddler learns to read, and therefore respect, the water. Nobody ever really beats whitewater. Under that deep roar lies wild power that nothing can tame; it just toys with those who play with it, and graciously rewards those who know it with almost life-transcending moments. Then it allows both to paddle (or swim) to the bank and get out.

As I write, Jesus Christ has not returned and we must continue to live a life of faith amidst what a friend sarcastically calls the "goodies of existence." To all of us still in the stuff, I say embrace God with everything you have. Deeper than the thunder and the force of whitewater, He resonates throughout His being with a wild, fiery love that those who would rather stand on shore know nothing about. All who throw off every earthly security to embrace God will not be disappointed on at least three counts.

Boulders and Spray

All those who long to embrace God should expect boulders and whitewater. Sometimes God is better found in turbulence than in security; calm may be a stagnant backwater for the faithless. I have scraped and slid over boulders bigger than automobiles that I feared would flip us. I have ridden into the sky on waves that crashed icily over us and sucked us into holes that shot us into the air. Jesus never promised easy times for those following Him; Satan will guarantee hard times—boulders and whitewater.

When that happens, the person embracing God can expect something else: Jesus Christ will never fall out of the raft. Somehow five novices pinballed through class IV rapids on the upper Arkansas River without flipping, but the fear of no one in control destroyed the rest of the float.

Jesus Christ ascended to heaven leaving behind a few confused novices to advance the most important cause ever seen against the most vicious and powerful opposition imaginable. They wouldn't face it alone. One of the last things Jesus told them before He ascended was, "I am with you always, even to the end of the age" (Matthew 28:20).

He meant every word: When we embrace God in Jesus Christ, nothing will knock Him out or shake Him loose. Christ knows every crosscurrent and undertow of God's working, reading God's hand in every inch of channel that we find incomprehensible and threatening. He has also gotten hung on and wrapped around all the worst that Satan and his demons can throw in the way, yet He broke free. To embrace God is to embrace a conqueror in Jesus Christ.

The richest embraces that this conqueror knows are shared with the ones who fought by His side. Leave the dead security of shore to others. Plunge into the teeth of life in Christ with all its struggles and challenges. You will never spend a second alone in the whitewater; your Guide knows the love and power of God like the back of His hand, as well as every wile of our fiercest enemy. Nothing can shake Him from our side.

A Final Promise

One final promise for those who embrace God: You are in for the ride of your life. The ministry team of youth I mentioned earlier worked harder physically and spiritually than they ever had before. When it was over, I asked them one question: Was it worth it? Their eyes teared and they were too choked up to speak, but they all nodded yes.

In heaven we will join with others who made every kind of sacrifice, endured every kind of deprivation and suffering, and lived through every kind of abuse and torture. As we stand before Christ's throne ablaze in His righteousness, we will say, from every corner of the globe and in every language, that embracing Him was worth it.

"The Spirit and the bride say 'Come!' And let the one who hears say 'Come!' And let the one who is thirsty come; let the one who wishes take the water of life without cost" (Revelation 22:17). The weeping, broken, burdened heart of God cries "Come!" while a dying world shuffles its guilty feet on the shoreline.

Others may hold back, stick a toe in the water, or splash around with one bare foot to test the temperature. But let us plunge into God's grace and love that sweeps away into life abundant and eternal. Then we will disappear among the boulders and foam into Christ's embrace that stands open and will never close until we are safely enfolded in its depths.

Notes

1. Quoted in David Watson, *Called and Committed* (Wheaton, IL: Harold Shaw, 1982), p. 189.
2. George Mallone, *Arming for Spiritual Warfare* (Downers Grove, IL: InterVarsity Press, 1991), p. 161.
3. Eugene Peterson, *Run with the Horses* (Downers Grove, IL: InterVarsity Press, 1983), p. 50.
4. Field Marshal Montgomery, *The Path to Leadership* (New York: G.P. Putnam & Sons, 1961), p. 115.
5. Charles Colson, *The Body: Being Light in Darkness* (Dallas: Word Publishing, 1992), p. 390.
6. Richard Lovelace, *Dynamics of Spiritual Life: An Evangelical Theology of Renewal* (Downers Grove, IL: InterVarsity Press, 1979), p. 88.
7. Michael Green, *You Must Be Joking: Popular Excuses for Avoiding Jesus Christ* (Wheaton, IL: Tyndale House Publishers, 1976), p. 35.
8. Peterson, *Run with the Horses*, p. 186.
9. A. W. Tozer quoted in David Watson, *I Believe in Evangelism* (Grand Rapids, MI: William B. Eerdmans Publishers, 1976), p. 185.
10. J. I. Packer, *Knowing God* (Downers Grove, IL: InterVarsity Press, 1973), pp. 95-96.
11. Henri J. M. Nouwen, *Reaching Out: The Three Movements of the Spiritual Life* (Garden City, NY: Doubleday and Company, 1975), p. 30.
12. Frederick Buechner, *Wishful Thinking: A Theological ABC* (San Francisco: Harper and Row, 1973), p. 28.
13. C. S. Lewis, *Reflections on the Psalms* (New York: Harcourt Brace Jovanovich Publishers, 1958), pp. 94-95.
14. Eugene H. Peterson, *The Message: The New Testament in Contemporary English* (Colorado Springs: NavPress, 1993), p. 414 (Philippians 2:5-8).
15. Ibid., p. 29 (Matthew 10:38,39).
16. Ibid., p. 43 (Matthew 16:25,26).
17. Ibid., p. 21 (Matthew 6:28-34).
18. Jean Vanier, *From Brokenness to Community* (Mahwah, NJ: Paulist Press, 1992), p. 48.
19. Kenneth S. Kantzer, "What Happens When Koreans Pray," in *Christianity Today*, Aug. 16, 1993, p. 13.
20. Clyde E. Fant Jr. and William M. Pinson Jr., *Twenty Centuries of Great Preaching* (Waco, TX: Word Books, Inc., 1971), vol. XI, p. 58.

Other Good Harvest House Reading

NEAR TO THE HEART OF GOD
by *Deborah Kern*

God wants us to pray. And He created prayer in such a way that a consistent, life-changing prayer experience would not be out of anyone's reach. Deborah Kern's thoughtful chapters and down-to-earth illustrations shed light on even the hard-to-understand aspects of prayer, including prayers that go unanswered and what to do when you just can't pray. Wherever you are in prayer—whether you've been praying for years or are just starting out—this book will bring freshness and renewed enthusiasm to your prayer life.

THE INTERNATIONAL INDUCTIVE STUDY BIBLE

Most Christians have been encouraged to study the Word of God, yet many have never been shown how. *The International Inductive Study Bible* teaches you clearly and simply how to unearth the treasures of God's Word by leading you directly back to the source—allowing God's Word to become its own commentary.

THE DAILY BIBLE
New International Version
Compiled by *F. LaGard Smith*

Unlike any other Bible you have ever read, *The Daily Bible* allows you to read the Scriptures chronologically as a powerful, uninterrupted account of God's interaction with human history.

You will see events from Creation through Revelation unfold before you like an epic novel, conveniently organized into 365 sections for daily reading. Gain a better overall perspective of Scripture by reading the Bible in the order the events occurred from the widely acclaimed New International Version.

MEETING GOD IN QUIET PLACES
by *F. LaGard Smith*

When the clamor of life threatens to overwhelm you, come share a quiet moment of peaceful intimacy with the Father in *Meeting God in Quiet Places*. These 30 sensitive parables from nature, drawn from bestselling author F. LaGard Smith's reflections in the Cotswold region of England, will refresh both your eye and soul. With illustrative pencil-sketch drawings by English artist Glenda Rae, this special book is one you'll return to throughout the year for life-renewing insights to guide you to the very heart of God.

SILENT STRENGTH FOR MY LIFE
by *Lloyd John Ogilvie*

Gladness . . . refreshment . . . encouragement . . . renewal . . . these are the rich rewards of quiet time spent with God. Daily time spent with God, alone in His presence, satisfied by His Word, makes our hearts stronger and our vision clearer. *Silent Strength* is designed to help you maximize your time with our Lord. As we glimpse His power, we find ourselves ready to meet the challenges of the day with a strength that is beyond our own, a silent strength that comes from God alone.

HIS IMPRINT, MY EXPRESSION
by *Kay Arthur*

The breathtaking, transforming power of a moment-by-moment relationship with Jesus Christ is portrayed in topical devotions by internationally recognized communicator and Bible teacher Kay Arthur. More than a devotional, *His Imprint, My Expression* is an intimate journey for those who long to be shaped by the Master's hand. Like a friend, Kay speaks directly to the broken, the wounded, and the hurting. Through times of disappointment and discouragement as well as times of renewal and rejoicing, Kay shows readers how to let the pressures of life press them into the likeness of Christ.

EVERY DAY WITH JESUS
by *Greg Laurie*

Pastor and evangelist Greg Laurie explores intimate relationship with Jesus in daily devotions based on the Gospel of Luke. Stories and word pictures offer life-renewing lessons gleaned from Jesus' interactions with people who walked in company with Him day by day. *Every Day with Jesus* overflows with practical insights and motivation to live every day as an adventure and a celebration.

Dear Reader:

We would appreciate hearing from you regarding this Harvest House nonfiction book. It will enable us to continue to give you the best in Christian publishing.

1. What most influenced you to purchase *Embracing God*?
   - ☐ Author
   - ☐ Subject matter
   - ☐ Backcover copy
   - ☐ Recommendations
   - ☐ Cover/Title
   - ☐ _____

2. Where did you purchase this book?
   - ☐ Christian bookstore
   - ☐ General bookstore
   - ☐ Department store
   - ☐ Grocery store
   - ☐ Other

3. Your overall rating of this book:
   ☐ Excellent   ☐ Very good   ☐ Good   ☐ Fair   ☐ Poor

4. How likely would you be to purchase other books by this author?
   - ☐ Very likely
   - ☐ Somewhat likely
   - ☐ Not very likely
   - ☐ Not at all

5. What types of books most interest you? (check all that apply)
   - ☐ Women's Books
   - ☐ Marriage Books
   - ☐ Current Issues
   - ☐ Self-Help/Psychology
   - ☐ Bible Studies
   - ☐ Fiction
   - ☐ Biographies
   - ☐ Children's Books
   - ☐ Youth Books
   - ☐ Other _____

6. Please check the box next to your age group.
   - ☐ Under 18
   - ☐ 18-24
   - ☐ 25-34
   - ☐ 35-44
   - ☐ 45-54
   - ☐ 55 and over

Mail to: Editorial Director
Harvest House Publishers
1075 Arrowsmith
Eugene, OR 97402

Name _____

Address _____

City _____ State _____ Zip _____

**Thank you for helping us to help you
in future publications!**